Cut Foliage

A practical guide to its selection and care

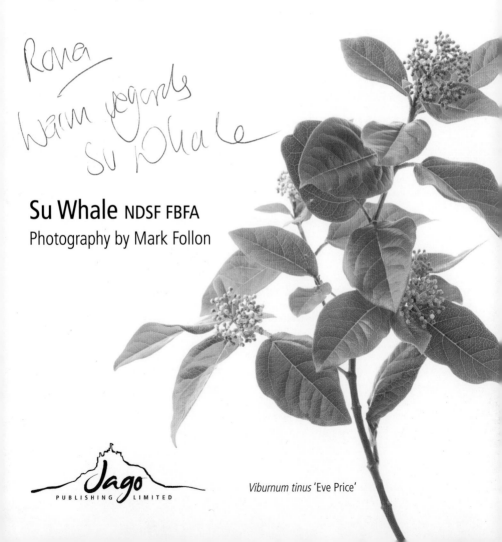

Su Whale NDSF FBFA

Photography by Mark Follon

Jago
PUBLISHING LIMITED

Viburnum tinus 'Eve Price'

Published by:

Jago Publishing Ltd.
23 Tomlan Road
West Heath
Birmingham
B31 3NX

info@jagopublishing.co.uk
www.jagopublishing.co.uk

First Published 2013

A CIP catalogue record for this book is available from the British Library.

ISBN 978-0-9568713-1-2

Designed by Corner House Design and Print Ltd, Manchester.

Printed in England by Coloprint Ltd, Birmingham.

Contents

Typha angustifolia

Introduction

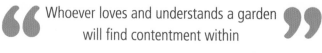
When my first book 'Cut Flowers A practical guide to their selection and care' was published, the second question (after, 'wow, how long did that take you to write?') was 'will there be a foliage book to go with it?' Having always worked on the principle of saying 'yes' to everything, and then working out how to do it afterwards I promised a foliage follow-up. Just over two years later, here it is.

For non-flower people (shame on you), producing a book on what appears on the surface to be nothing but leaves and twigs might seem a little idiosyncratic, and I will be the first to admit that foliage doesn't have the pulling power of flowers, but where would we be without it?

How would arrangements and vases turn out with no greenery to give support, shape and contrast? Imagine no garlanding at weddings, no fabulous constructions filling huge public spaces at flower festivals, no gorgeous autumn designs filled with the season's rich colours, no holly at Christmas!

I rest my case.

Floristry students I know need to study foliage for their course work and I hope this book will be of use to them, it will also hopefully be a handy reference for florists and flower arrangers. But, as with 'Cut Flowers' I would love to think that anyone who has an interest in flowers, who simply likes to arrange them at home for their own pleasure will find this book of use – and if it encourages people to pop into their local high street florist to buy foliage along with their flowers – then I will be more than happy.

Enjoy your flowers!

SuWhale

Cut flowers and foliage in the home

Why use foliage?
Foliage is an essential component when you have flowers in the home, if only for the reason that it will help to fill out your vase, making your flower arrangement look bigger and more impressive! It can also help to hold flowers in position and many foliage's will last longer than flowers, so they can be reused more than once.

Using foliage straight from the garden
Having a garden full of shrubs is perfect for the keen flower arranger, however, when using garden foliage avoid cutting new growth as it does not have the robustness or longevity of more mature foliage. If using in competition/commercial work, it is advisable to cut foliage the day before so that it can be conditioned overnight.

Good housekeeping
When it comes down to the basics, the needs of fresh cut flowers and foliage is very much like ours– they need water, fresh air and food to keep healthy. Bear these facts in mind and there is no reason why you shouldn't be able to enjoy your flowers for their maximum vase life. Longevity is helped by good hygiene, wash vases thoroughly after use (not just emptying them out and putting them back in the cupboard – we've all done it!) This is important, as bacteria inside grubby vases can pollute the water and shorten your flower and foliage life.

Water
Use clean, fresh water. How much water in the vase depends on its size, but approximately two thirds is about right. If you have an opaque vase, don't forget to top it up!

Re-cutting stems
This is the single most important way to keep your flowers and foliage healthy. Out of water stem ends will seal over as they dry out, so always re-cut dry stems before placing in your vase. Over time stems can become blocked with bacteria which reduce their ability to take up water. It is well worth every few days refreshing the water and re-cutting about 2cm (1") off the bottom of stems, this will make a huge difference to their vase life.

Always re-cut stems at an angle, (unless they are hollow in which case they should be left flat) this exposes a larger area to absorb water and means the stem ends aren't sitting on the base of the container. (Please don't bash/split or crush woody stems – it just mashes up vital capillaries which are responsible for taking water up to the flower head)

Foliage v Water
Do remove all foliage in contact with water, left on, it will decay and pollute the water, shortening your flower's vase life.

Flower Food
All flowers and foliage need clean water and most of them need feeding as well. Commercial flower food has been developed to meet both of those needs; it will keep bacteria at bay and provide necessary nutrients. 'Home grown' remedies such as using bleach, copper pennies or aspirin do part of that job, but not all of it. (Bleach should be avoided as it can burn the stems and leaves).

Displaying at home
Fresh flowers and foliage don't enjoy being in direct heat, so keep them away from radiators and out of direct sunlight – a cool spot with good air circulation is ideal.

How to use this book

A page has been devoted to each foliage, laid out in the same order for ease of reference.

Botanical Name: Foliage is arranged in alphabetical order of botanical names.

Common Name: The most popular name/names by which the foliage is commonly known.

Availability: The availability of commercially cut foliage is taken largely from the Flower Council of Holland (FCH). The Netherlands are the world's biggest exporter of cut flowers and foliage, so this is most likely where your florist or wholesaler will be sourcing them from. It has generally been assumed that garden grown evergreen shrubs are available all year round – see page 5 for more information on cutting garden foliage.

Vase Life: The typical life of the foliage if conditioned correctly and kept in optimum conditions either in the flower shop or at home.

Foliage Notes: A short paragraph to give some general background to the foliage. Where the botanical name is a little tricky, I have included a guide to pronunciation. This paragraph also includes stem length. Wary that eyes tend to glaze over when numbers are involved, I have used short, medium and tall instead. As actual measurements they are as follows:

Short stem length: 10cm–30cm (4"–12") e.g. Galax up to Hosta.

Medium stem length: 30cm–55cm (12"–22") e.g. Hosta up to Aspidistra.

Tall/Long stem length: 55cm–90cm (22"–36") e.g. Aspidistra up to Strelitzia and above. 'Long' refers specifically to trailing foliage.

Colour Range: Based on the accepted descriptions of different shades of green (with a little poetic licence).

Conditioning & General Information: Any particular points relevant to the foliage, such as if it's woody stemmed. These sections also include:

Leaf shape: These can be crossed referenced with leaf shapes in visual form which can be found in 'A mini foliage miscellany' on page 151.

Texture: Based on both visual and actual texture. As texture is open to interpretation, I have tried to keep it as straightforward as possible, but I accept that there are cases where my description may not be the same as someone else's!

In Design and Wedding Work:
Suggestions on how the foliage can be used in designs, plus its suitability for wedding work which also includes whether or not it can be wired. This is to help students, florists and flower arrangers in their choice of foliage and is based on over twenty years in commercial floristry so by definition is slightly subjective – feel free to experiment! This is also where I have included foliage meaning if there is one.

For Students:
Family and genus: Plant groups are often being reclassified as more becomes known about their botanical make-up. Where there has been conflicting information, I have used the Royal Horticultural Society (RHS) as a benchmark. The abbreviation 'sp' indicates where there is more than one species within the genus commonly used in floristry.
Origin: Where the foliage is native to, not necessarily where it has now naturalised.
Trivia: Amazing what you can learn!

How to use this book

Symbols:

 Aromatic Foliage with a noticeable (pleasant!) scent such as Eucalyptus.

 Bunches How the foliage is bought or is available to buy, either by florists via wholesalers, or customers. Bunches are nearly always in multiples of 5.

 Can be dried This foliage can be preserved at home by drying.

 Grows in the garden This applies to any shrubs etc. that are commonly found growing in gardens.

 Houseplant It is possible to obtain this foliage as a houseplant from either your local florist or garden centre.

 Irritant/Prickly This is where either the sap or the foliage itself can have an irritant quality or it has sharp thorns or spines.

 Poisonous Always wash hands and clean workbenches/tables after handling poisonous foliage.

 Pungent flower Foliage with a scent which is not necessarily fragrant, such as Allium.

 Single Stem How a customer could expect to buy the foliage from a florist – this would be from a bunch broken down into individual stems.

 Weight Some foliage is sold by weight, such as mistletoe and holly.

And finally… the foliage symbol. Next to the botanical name of each foliage is a small green outline of a leaf. This is to give the reader an indication of the size of the foliage in real life compared to the photograph in the book.

Many of the photographs are actual size which is indicated thus:

Half actual size of photograph

Twice the size

And so on!

7

Abies

Common Name: **Noble fir**

Availability: November–December.

Vase Life: 14–21 days.

Foliage Notes: Pronounced 'A-bees'. Traditional Christmas evergreen with stiff, dense foliage completely covering its branches. Medium/tall stem length.

Colour Range: Blue-green.

Abies procera (Syn. *Abies nobilis*)

Conditioning:

- Ideal temperature range: 2–5°C (36–41°F).
- Sold in bundles which can be stored outside until needed.
- If kept inside store in a refrigerated room.
- Spray with water occasionally to prevent foliage from drying out.
- Store away from direct heat and draughts.

General Information:

- Use secateurs to cut branches and condition before use in fresh water.
- Use a knife to chamfer the end of the stem to make it easier to insert into floral foam.
- **Texture:** Spiky.
- **Leaf shape:** Needle.
- **Would complement:** Christmas flowers; Hippeastrum, Hellebores, ivy and holly.

In Design and Wedding Work:

Known by many florists as 'blue spruce' this long-lasting foliage is perfect for seasonal arrangements and door wreaths. Indispensable for Christmas weddings, as not only is it reliable but it smells great as well! Add into table arrangements and wreaths; larger pieces can be used as backing for festive wall swags, door decorations and pedestal designs. It can be added into bridal tieds and shower bouquets if the stems are cleaned properly first, but watch out for the sticky resin.

Foliage meaning: Elevation.

For Students:

Family: Pinaceae.

Genus & Species: *Abies procera*.

Native to: N/W America.

Trivia: First introduced into the UK from America in 1830, the tallest Noble Fir in this country is reputed to be at Taymouth Castle in Perthshire, standing at an impressive 47m (160').

Acacia

Availability: July–February, peaks September–February.

Vase Life: 10–14 days.

Foliage Notes: Pronounced 'A-CASE-sia.' A sturdy, woody stemmed ornamental shrub with delicate, fern-like leaves and bright yellow flowers. Medium stem length.

Colour Range: Silvery-grey with a touch of purple.

Conditioning:

- Ideal temperature range: 2–5°C (36–41°F).
- Re-cut stems at an angle, preferably with secateurs.
- Stand in shallow water which should be topped up every day.
- Store away from direct heat and draughts.
- Remove foliage in contact with water.

General Information:

- Has tiny thorns, handle with care.
- Suitable for using in floral foam, ensure containers are kept topped up with water.
- **Texture:** Feathery.
- **Leaf shape:** Pinnate.
- **Would complement:** Spring flowers, especially those in blue/lemon/purple shades.

Acacia baileyana 'Purpurea'

In Design and Wedding Work:

Due to its bushy habit Acacia is a handy filler foliage. Cut into small pieces to fill gaps in loose funeral work and for edging tributes. The delicate appearance of Acacia will also add a softness to traditional designs. It lasts well in floral foam but is too untidy to have prominence in modern arrangements. Acacia stems are a little too stiff for informal wedding work.

Foliage Meaning: Friendship.

For Students:

Family: Mimosaceae.

Genus & Species: *Acacia baileyana*.

Native to: Majority from Australia.

Trivia: The Golden Wattle, *Acacia pycnantha* is Australia's national floral emblem. September 1st is Wattle Day.

Aglaonema

Common Name: **Chinese evergreen**

Availability: All year round.

Vase Life: 7–10 days.

Foliage Notes: Pronounced 'Ag-leo-neema'. A tropical perennial whose natural habitats are swamps and rain forests. Sold in mixed bunches of tropical green leaves. Short stem length.

Colour Range: Emerald green with cream variegation.

Conditioning:

- Ideal temperature range: 12–15°C (54–59°F).
- Re-cut stems with scissors.
- Stand in clean, shallow water with flower food.
- Change water every 2–3 days.
- Store away from direct heat and draughts, humidity is important.
- Don't overcrowd containers as leaves can rot without sufficient air circulation.

General Information:

- Aglaonema can be an irritant, so always wash hands after use.
- Soft stemmed, so handle with care. Wire stems before inserting into floral foam.
- **Texture:** Smooth.
- **Leaf Shape:** Lance.
- **Would complement:** Tropical flowers such as Curcuma, Anthurium and Zantedeschia.

In Design and Wedding Work:

This attractive tropical foliage can be rolled and pinned to make an edging for modern, linear style hand-tied designs and can also be used as focal foliage in contemporary arrangements. In wedding work, the interesting, patterned leaves will provide a contrast to bolder flowers in either traditional or modern designs. Use to give a dramatic outline in vases but steer away from tied bridal work as the sap from the leaf can irritate, although it could be used in shower bouquets designed in holders.

 Aglaonema commutatum

For Students:

Family: Araceae.

Genus & Species: *Aglaonema commutatum*.

Native to: S/E Asia.

Trivia: Aglaonema is regarded as a good omen in Asia; some even count the dots on the leaves which they then convert into lottery numbers.

Common Name: **Serpent garlic**

Availability: April–August.

Vase Life: 10–15 days.

Foliage Notes: An unusual member of the Allium family with a leafless, coiled stem. Used commercially for its interesting shape. Medium stem length.

Colour Range: Bright green.

Conditioning:

- Ideal temperature range: 6–10°C (43–50°F).
- Re-cut stems, preferably with a knife.
- Stand in clean water with flower food.
- Change water every 2–3 days.
- Store away from direct heat and draughts.

General Information:

- Suitable for both vase designs and floral foam.
- A member of the onion family, it can give off a strong odour when cut.
- Don't overcrowd containers or vases to avoid tangling stems.
- **Texture:** Smooth.
- **Would complement:** Tall flowers; Liatris, Ornithogalum, Anthurium.

In Design and Wedding Work:
Use in contemporary, linear style hand-tied designs to make the most of its fascinating form. It is also excellent for vegetative, natural arrangements. It would be an interesting addition to wedding flowers – although possibly not something that you would expect to see in bridal work! Its unusual outline would suit contemporary vase designs or arrangements in floral foam and would look particularly effective in a modern setting.

 Allium sativum ophioscorodon

For Students:
Family: Alliaceae.
Genus & Species: *Allium sativum.*
Native to: Central Asia.
Trivia: Allium has many uses; it is possible, for example, to make glue from garlic bulbs which is then used to mend glass and china.

11

Alocasia

Common Name: **Elephant ear, African mask**

Availability: All year round.

Vase Life: 5–7 days.

Foliage Notes: Pronounced 'Alo-KAY-sia'. A striking tropical plant which grows from underground corms. A popular hothouse conservatory plant. Short stem length.

Colour Range: Dark green with creamy white veins.

Conditioning:

- Ideal temperature range: 12–15°C (54–59°F).
- If using a plant, store Alocasia in a warm, light, draft free spot.
- Cut leaves from the main stem with care, using scissors.
- Stand in clean shallow water with a small amount of flower food.
- Change water every 2–3 days.

General Information:

- Store away from direct heat and draughts, mist leaves lightly.
- **Texture:** Ribbed.
- **Leaf Shape:** Spear.
- **Would complement:** Tropical flowers; Curcuma, Zantedeschia, Protea.

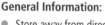 *Alocasia x amazonica* Polly

In Design and Wedding Work:
Despite being soft stemmed Alocasia is strong enough for using in floral foam and is perfect for contemporary design work; arrange it in groups where it will have more impact. With such a distinctive pattern it needs to be shown off in bridal designs. It will give a dramatic backing to boutonnières and corsages; it would also be very effective in modern shower bouquets.

For Students:
Family: Araceae.

Genus & Species: *Alocasia x amazonica*.

Native to: Tropical Asia.

Trivia: It is claimed that the term 'Amazonica' was coined by American nursery owner Salvadore Mauro who, in the 1950's, named the plant after his own nursery business.

Ananas

Common Name: Dwarf pink pineapple, Decorative pineapple, Curagua

Availability: March–November.

Vase Life: 7–10 days.

Foliage Notes: An ornamental pineapple with tough leaves that grow into an attractive rosette. Can be grown as a houseplant under the right conditions. Short/medium stem length.

Colour Range: Pink, yellow, pale green.

Conditioning:

- Ideal temperature range: 12–15°C (54–59°F).
- Re-cut stems at an angle preferably with secateurs.
- Stand in clean water, flower food is not necessary.
- Change water every 4–5 days.
- Store away from direct heat and draughts which can turn the foliage brown.

General Information:

- Handle with care, heads can be knocked off easily.
- Use secateurs to cut the woody stems.
- **Texture:** Rough.
- **Leaf Shape:** Strap like with sawtooth edges.
- **Would complement:** Tropical flowers; Heliconia, Strelitzia and Anthurium.

 *Ananas lucidus*

In Design and Wedding Work:

When using in floral foam ensure the fruits are not touching wet surfaces. They are top heavy, so place them low in the centre of designs. Ananas is not on many brides' wish list but would be perfect for a tropical theme. Use them for a beach wedding party or for a welcome reception for brides who have married abroad. Combine with bold foliage and similar tropical flowers for a fun and quirky design.

Foliage meaning: You are perfect.

For Students:

Family: Bromeliaceae.

Genus & Species: *Ananas lucidus*.

Native to: Venezuela & Ecuador.

Trivia: In the Philippines, the leaves of the edible pineapple (*A. comosus*) are used as a source of textile fibre which is often found in wallpaper.

Availability: All year round.

Vase Life: 14–21 days.

Foliage Notes: A tropical evergreen with attractive heart-shaped leaves which grow singly on slim, straight stems. Medium stem length.

Colour Range: Dark glossy green.

Conditioning:

- Ideal temperature range: 12–15°C (54–59°F).
- Re-cut stems at an angle, preferably with a knife.
- Stand in clean water with flower food.
- Change water every 4–5 days.
- Store away from direct heat and draughts.

General Information:

- Long-lasting foliage suitable for using in both vase designs and floral foam.
- Can apply leaf shine to give a glossy look.
- **Texture:** Smooth.
- **Leaf Shape:** Heart.
- **Would complement:** Tropical flowers; Anthurium (of course!) Protea and Curcuma.

x2 *Anthurium andraeanum*

In Design and Wedding Work:
Distinctive enough to be used as focal foliage; Anthurium will also make an attractive edging for modern, linear style hand-tieds. Include it in both traditional and modern wedding work although the smaller leaves may get a little lost in larger arrangements. In bridal designs, Anthurium will make an interesting collar around contemporary tied posies and would be very effective in modern shower bouquets.

For Students:
Family: Araceae.
Genus & Species: *Anthurium andraeanum*.
Native to: Central & S. America.
Trivia: In drier climates Anthurium leaves are capable of forming a rosette shape in order to collect vital water and nutrients.

Arachniodes

Common Name: **Leather leaf, Leather fern**

Availability: All year round.

Vase Life: 14–28 days.

Foliage Notes: Pronounced 'Arack-NOY-dees'. This versatile fern can be seen as old-fashioned, although its robustness and longevity shouldn't be underestimated. Medium stem length.

Colour Range: Dark green.

Conditioning:

- Ideal temperature range: 2–5°C (36–41°F).
- Stand in clean water with flower food.
- Change water every 4–5 days, keeping fronds out of contact with water.
- Store away from direct heat and draughts, humidity is important.
- Dries out easily, spray lightly daily and keep loosely wrapped in plastic.

General Information:

- Spores on the underside of mature leaves can produce a brown dust.
- Can snap easily, so handle with care.
- **Texture:** Lacy.
- **Leaf Shape:** Bipinnate.
- **Would complement:** Large headed, traditional flowers.

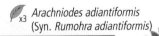 *Arachniodes adiantiformis*
(Syn. *Rumohra adiantiformis*)

In Design and Wedding Work:

Suitable for using in both vase designs and floral foam and excellent for foliage edging funeral work and for defining outlines, it will also make an attractive collar for hand-ties. Leather leaf used to be very popular in wedding work to edge bridal posies and back shower bouquets, but with trends moving towards more natural styling it is now seen as being a little too 'stiff' for bridal work, although it is still a useful and inexpensive foliage for pedestal designs and arrangements. Can be wired with care.

For Students:

Family: Dryopteriadaceae.

Genus & Species: *Arachniodes adiantiformis*.

Native to: Asia.

Trivia: The name 'adianton' means 'unwettable' referring to the fronds ability to shed water.

Arbutus

Common Name: **Strawberry tree, Cane apple**

Availability: Peaks February–May, July–September.

Vase Life: 14–21 days.

Foliage Notes: A popular evergreen shrub with small white flowers in autumn followed by edible, strawberry-like fruits in the autumn of the following year. Medium stem length.

Colour Range: Green with a red tinge.

Conditioning:

- Ideal temperature range: 2–5°C (36–41°F).
- Re-cut stems, preferably with secateurs.
- Stand in clean, shallow water, flower food is not necessary.
- Change water every 4–5 days.
- Store away from direct heat and draughts.

General Information:

- Hardy, tough leaves with slightly toothed edges. Woody stemmed.
- Long-lasting foliage suitable for using in both vase designs and floral foam.
- **Texture:** Bushy.
- **Leaf Shape:** Oval.
- **Would complement:** Traditional style garden flowers; Leucanthemum, Kniphofia, Rubeckia.

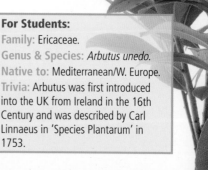

Arbutus unedo f. *rubra*

In Design and Wedding Work:
A dense foliage, Arbutus is very useful in funeral work, in particular for foliage edging and adding texture and bulk in loose tributes. A little too bushy for streamlined modern designs although ideal for filling out large pedestal style arrangements. Arbutus could be considered for natural bridal tied bouquets, in which case choose an autumn wedding which is when its fruits and leaf colour are at their best.
Foliage meaning: Esteem and love.

For Students:
Family: Ericaceae.
Genus & Species: *Arbutus unedo*.
Native to: Mediterranean/W. Europe.
Trivia: Arbutus was first introduced into the UK from Ireland in the 16th Century and was described by Carl Linnaeus in 'Species Plantarum' in 1753.

Common Name: **Smilax, Bridal creeper, Bridal veil creeper**

Availability: All year round, peaks June–August.

Vase Life: 7–10 days.

Foliage Notes: A climbing plant with twisting, wiry stems that can grow up to 3m (10') long. Scrambles easily though trees and large shrubs. Long stem length.

Colour Range: Green.

Conditioning:

- Ideal temperature range: 2–5°C (36–41°F).
- Smilax is normally packaged in long lengths and wrapped in plastic.
- Leave the foliage in its wrapping until needed. Recut the stem end and place in water.
- Store away from direct heat and draughts.
- Needs high humidity to prevent it from drying out.

General Information:

- Can be pinned into floral foam or used in large vase designs.
- **Texture:** Bushy.
- **Leaf shape:** Ovate.
- **Would complement:** Great for garlanding and swags.

Asparagus asparagoides
(Syn. *Asparagus medeoloides*)

In Design and Wedding Work:

Smilax used to be very popular in wedding work but has fallen out of favour in recent years. Very flexible so an excellent foliage for garlanding, although it can work out quite costly if large amounts are required. Showy cascade designs and table swaging are also areas where smilax can be relied on, but handle with care as it has prickly spines! A candidate for large, showy bridal shower bouquets, but not suitable for wiring.

For Students:

Family: Asparagaceae.

Genus & Species: *Asparagus asparagoides*.

Native to: South Africa.

Trivia: *A. asparagoides* has been used in bridal bouquets since the mid-19th Century when it was first introduced into Europe from South Africa.

17

Asparagus

Common Name: **Foxtail fern, Plume Asparagus**

Availability: All year round.

Vase Life: 7–14 days.

Foliage Notes: A bushy perennial with erect stems covered with tiny soft branches. Pinkish white flowers in spring are followed by red berries in summer. Medium stem length.

Colour Range: Emerald green.

Conditioning:

- Ideal temperature range: 2–5°C (36–41°F).
- Re-cut stems with scissors.
- Handle with caution; there are spines on the stem which are extremely sharp.
- Change water every 4–5 days and store away from direct heat and draughts.
- Stand in clean water with flower food.
- Needs high humidity to prevent it from drying out which causes foliage drop.

General Information:

- Suitable for using in both vase designs and floral foam.
- Cut off sharp spines with scissors.
- **Texture:** Feathery.
- **Would complement:** Gerberas, carnations or Helianthus.

x3 *Asparagus densiflorus* 'Myersii'
(Syn. *Asparagus aethiopicus* 'Myersii')

In Design and Wedding Work:
It has a tendency to dry out quickly so if using in floral foam always keep the container well topped up and spray arrangements regularly. Popular for giving line and height to designs, it can be used in either traditional or contemporary work. Seen as a little old-fashioned for weddings, although it can be very useful in large pedestal designs or smaller, showy venue arrangements. Not suitable for wired work.

For Students:
Family: Asparagaceae.

Genus & Species: *Asparagus densiflorus*.

Native to: South Africa.

Trivia: The Pied Currawong bird is one of the chief culprits in spreading the seeds of Plume asparagus around Sydney Australia where it is seen as an invasive weed.

Asparagus

Common Name: **Basket Asparagus, Emerald feather**

Availability: All year round.

Vase Life: 7–14 days.

Foliage Notes: A bushy perennial with a naturally trailing habit, its needle-like 'leaves' are actually tiny branches, the leaves inconspicuous scales. Medium stem length.

Colour Range: Emerald green.

Conditioning:

- Ideal temperature range: 2–5°C (36–41°F).
- Re-cut stems with scissors.
- Foliage can turn yellow if stored in the dark for long periods.
- Change water every 4–5 days, and store away from direct heat and draughts.
- Stand in clean water with flower food.
- Needs high humidity to prevent it from drying out.

General Information:

- Suitable for using in both vase designs and floral foam.
- Cut off any sharp spines that will be in contact with skin using a pair of scissors.
- **Texture:** Feathery.
- **Would complement:** Delicate flowers; spray carnations, Aster or Helenium

Asparagus densiflorus 'Sprengeri' (Syn. *Asparagus aethiopicus* 'Sprengeri')

In Design and Wedding Work:

Always keep containers well topped up and spray arrangements regularly as the foliage has a tendency to drop. A bushy foliage, Sprengeri will fill out hand-tieds and arrangements and is best suited for traditional work rather than contemporary design. In wedding work its trailing habit makes it very useful for cascade bouquets and for adding volume to large arrangements. Not suitable for wiring as it dries out too quickly.

For Students:

Family: Asparagaceae.

Genus & Species: *Asparagus densiflorus* 'Sprengeri'.

Native to: South Africa.

Trivia: Sprengeri can grow up to 2m (6') tall; its weeping habit makes it popular for hanging baskets in warm climates.

Asparagus

Common Name: **Lace fern, Plumosa, Climbing Asparagus**

Availability: All year round.

Vase Life: 10–14 days.

Foliage Notes: An evergreen climber which, despite its appearance, is not a true fern. Has flat, fine feathery foliage on wiry stems. Tall stem length.

Colour Range: Moss green.

Conditioning:

- Ideal temperature range: 2–5°C (36–41°F).
- Re-cut stems removing white ends as they will not take up water.
- Handle with care; spines on the stem are extremely sharp.
- Change water every 4–5 days, store away from direct heat and draughts.
- Stand in clean water with flower food.
- High humidity will help to prevent it drying out which can cause foliage drop.

General Information:

- Cut off sharp spines that will be in contact with skin using scissors.
- **Texture:** Feathery.
- **Would complement:** Carnations, roses, Chrysanthemum.

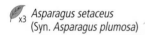

Asparagus setaceus
(Syn. *Asparagus plumosa*)

In Design and Wedding Work:

Use Asparagus fern to add drama to designs, its wiry trails will soften arrangements and 'blur' hard edges. Asparagus fern is traditionally the first choice for backing carnation buttonholes, but its use in wedding work goes beyond that. It will add a soft, delicate edging to tied posies or can be used to trail dramatically from shower bouquets. Visually it will add extra depth to large venue designs. Beware of the sharp spines if using in tied posies. Suitable for wiring.

For Students:

Family: Asparagaceae.

Genus & Species: *Asparagus setaceus*.

Native to: South Africa.

Trivia: *A. setaceus* grows as a vine in its natural state and can reach several meters in height. It is considered as an invasive weed in many parts of the world.

Asparagus

Common Name: **Ming fern, Zigzag fern**

Availability: All year round.

Vase Life: 10–14 days.

Foliage Notes: A woody evergreen shrub with a soft fluffy appearance although this is deceptive as the stems are covered in sharp spines. Medium stem length.

Colour Range: Emerald green.

Conditioning:

- Ideal temperature range: 2–5°C (36–41°F).
- Re-cut stems with scissors.
- Change water every 4–5 days and store away from direct heat and draughts.
- Has a tendency to shed foliage if left in a dry atmosphere.
- Needs humidity, spray lightly with water to prevent it from drying out.

General Information:

- Suitable for using in both vase designs and floral foam.
- Handle carefully; its spines are very sharp.
- **Texture:** Feathery.
- **Leaf Shape:** Needle.
- **Would complement:** Large headed, traditional flowers.

x2
Asparagus umbellatus

In Design and Wedding Work:

A handy foliage for bulking out hand-tied bouquets and vase designs, also for foliage edging funeral tributes. In wedding work this bushy Asparagus is very useful for using in large venue arrangements although it can also be cut into small pieces to add into table posies where its emerald green foliage will contrast brighter, more vivid flowers. Not recommended in natural tied posies due to its sharp spines although it can be used sparingly in wired work.

For Students:

Family: Asparagaceae.

Genus & Species: *Asparagus umbellatus*.

Native to: Macaronesia.

Trivia: Macaronesia is a group of volcanic islands in the North Atlantic which include The Azores and the Canary Islands.

Asparagus

Common Name: **Tree fern, Broom fern**

Availability: All year round.

Vase Life: 14–21 days.

Foliage Notes: A hardy, evergreen shrub with wiry branches that curve upwards with fine, needle-like, bushy foliage. Medium stem length.

Colour Range: Moss green.

Conditioning:

- Ideal temperature range: 2–5°C (36–41°F).
- Re-cut stems with scissors, removing white ends.
- Change water every 4–5 days and store away from direct heat and draughts.
- Adding flower food to the water is not necessary.
- *Asparagus virgatus* needs a humid atmosphere, spray lightly with water to prevent it from drying out.

General Information:

- Suitable for using in both vase designs and floral foam.
- **Texture:** Feathery.
- **Would complement:** Traditional flowers.

In Design and Wedding Work:
A filler foliage for hand-tied bouquets, it will also add a delicate softness to traditional arrangements but is too bushy for more contemporary work. *A. virgatus* has a light, feathery appearance, ideal for filling out designs, it is also good value for money – a little goes a long way! Its uses in bridal work are slightly more limited as it is not particularly attractive, but it is robust enough to use in wired work where it will add a soft outline to boutonnières and corsages. Include in garlanding and swags.

For Students:
Family: Asparagaceae.
Genus & Species: *Asparagus virgatus*.
Native to: Southern Africa.
Trivia: In its natural habitat, *Asparagus virgatus* is a shade loving species, which can be found growing in woodland and forest edges.

Asparagus virgatus ×2

Aspidistra

Availability: All year round.

Vase Life: 14–21 days.

Foliage Notes: A sturdy, reliable, evergreen perennial. Tolerant of neglect, Aspidistra is resilient with a bushy, upright habit. Medium/tall stem length.

Colour Range: Dark glossy green.

Conditioning:

- Ideal temperature range: 12–15°C (54–59°F).
- Re-cut stems, preferably with a knife.
- Stand in shallow water with flower food.
- Clean dirty leaves with a damp cloth.
- Store away from direct heat and draughts.

General Information:

- Use leaf shine to give Aspidistra an extra glossy look.
- Cut stems at an angle with a sharp knife.
- **Texture:** Smooth.
- **Leaf shape:** Elliptic.
- **Would complement:** Tall, bold flowers such as Allium, Hippeastrum and Chrysanthemum blooms.

x4 *Aspidistra elatior*

In Design and Wedding Work:

Aspidistra is real trooper; it gives length and visual weight to arrangements and can also be manipulated by splitting, rolling and pinning. Its large leaves can disguise floral foam in clear glass containers or be bound onto the exterior of tall vases. In wedding work it will provide solid backing and shape to large pedestal arrangements as well as a dramatic outline in table designs. Use to wrap around the stems of tied bridal posies as an alternative to ribbon, or as a rolled edge around more limited style bouquets.

For Students:

Family: Asparagaceae.

Genus & Species: *Aspidistra elatior*.

Native to: Far East.

Trivia: 'The Biggest Aspidistra in the World' was first sung by Gracie Fields in the 1938 British comedy film 'Keep Smiling'.

Aucuba

Common Name: **Japanese spotted laurel, Gold dust plant**

Availability: All year round.

Vase Life: 14–21 days.

Foliage Notes: Pronounced 'AWK-u-bah'. A hardy evergreen with leathery leaves covered in bright blotches. An attractive shrub grown for its ornamental appeal. Medium/tall stem length.

Colour Range: Emerald green, yellow.

Conditioning:

- Ideal temperature range: 2–5°C (36–41°F).
- Re-cut stems, preferably with a knife.
- Remove foliage below water level and stand in clean, fresh water.
- Change water every 4–5 days.
- Store away from direct heat and draughts.
- The attractive red berries are poisonous, keep away from children and inquisitive pets.

General Information:

- Long-lasting, suitable for using in vase designs and floral foam.
- Use a knife to cut stems at an angle to make it easier to insert into floral foam.
- **Texture:** Smooth/Glossy.
- **Leaf shape:** Elliptic.
- **Would complement:** Traditional flowers in a yellow/lime/orange colour scheme.

In Design and Wedding Work:

A great filler foliage for large arrangements and good for backing tied sheaves (in the appropriate colours!). Aucuba leaves can also be rolled and pinned and used in modern design work. With its bright green and yellow spotted leaves it wouldn't suit all colour schemes, but would be perfect for filling out large pedestal style designs and arrangements. The leaves are resilient and can be manipulated into more contemporary design work; suitable for wiring.

 Aucuba japonica 'Variegata'

For Students:

Family: Garryaceae.

Genus & Species: *Aucuba japonica*.

Native to: Japan & China.

Trivia: *A. japonica* was the first of the genus to reach Britain in the Nineteenth century from the Far East becoming a popular feature in Victorian shrubberies.

Bergenia

Common Name: **Elephant ear, Pig squeak**

Availability: April–November.

Vase Life: 14–21 days.

Foliage Notes: A popular evergreen perennial and good for ground cover, Bergenia has bright red, pink or white flowers which grow on short stems. Short stem length.

Colour Range: Mid-green, maturing to maroon in winter.

Conditioning:

- Ideal temperature range: 2–5°C (36–41°F).
- Re-cut stems, preferably with a knife.
- Stand in clean, shallow water.
- Change water every 4–5 days.
- Store away from direct heat and draughts.
- Needs a humid atmosphere to stop the leaves from drying out, can be stored outside.

General Information:

- Reliable foliage which can last up to three weeks in floral foam.
- **Texture:** Smooth.
- **Leaf Shape:** Heart.
- **Would complement:** Large headed flowers including Dahlia, peony and Hydrangea.

x2 *Bergenia cordifolia*

In Design and Wedding Work:

Bergenia is attractive foliage ideal for edging natural tied posies; it can also be used as focal foliage in garden style arrangements. A definite candidate for vintage style weddings where a 'just picked' look is required. The leaves are most suited to adding into table arrangements, their short stems will get a little lost in larger, pedestal style designs. Lovely for an autumn or winter wedding when the leaves naturally change colour to a deep mahogany.

For Students:

Family: Saxifragaceae.

Genus & Species: *Bergenia cordifolia*.

Native to: Central Asia.

Trivia: The common name 'pig squeak' derives from the sound that the leaves make when rubbed together.

Berzelia

Common Name: **Common buttonbush**

Availability: September–March.

Vase Life: 14–21 days.

Foliage Notes: Pronounced 'Ber-ZEE-lee-a'. A wiry evergreen covered in dense, needle-like leaves growing in spherical clusters in a tight group. Its creamy seeds can stay attached for up to two years. Medium stem length.

Colour Range: Bright green and grey with orange/brown tones.

Conditioning:

- Ideal temperature range: 5–10°C (41–50°F).
- Re-cut stems, preferably with a knife.
- Stand in clean, shallow water, flower food is not necessary.
- Change water every 4–5 days.
- Store away from direct heat and draughts.

Berzelia abrotanoides

General Information:

- Long-lasting foliage suitable for using in both vase designs and floral foam.
- **Texture:** Rounded/Spiky.
- **Leaf Shape:** Needle.
- **Would complement:** Textured flowers; Protea, Callistephus, Leucadendron.

Berzelia galpinii

In Design and Wedding Work:

Berzelia is often used as an ingredient in more exotic mixed bouquets (sometimes called safari bunches) alongside Protea and Brunia. Extremely long-lasting, it will add texture to hand-tied designs and arrangements although it is not significant enough a foliage to take centre stage. Available for autumn and winter weddings, it can be wired for buttonholes and boutonnières.

For Students:

Family: Bruniaceae.

Genus & Species: *Berzelia* sp.

Native to: South Africa.

Trivia: Berzelia was named in honour of Count Jacob Berzelius (1779-1845) a Swedish chemist who was the founder of chemical symbols.

Brachyglottis

Common Name: Ragwort sunshine, Daisy bush

Availability: All year round.

Vase Life: 14–21 days.

Foliage Notes: Pronounced 'Brack-e-glottis'. A shrub popular in landscaping schemes where its bright yellow flowers and distinctive foliage are a welcome splash of colour. Medium stem length.

Colour Range: Green with silvery-grey undersides.

Conditioning:

- Ideal temperature range: 2–5°C (36–41°F).
- Woody stemmed, re-cut at an angle with a sharp knife.
- Stand in clean water, flower food is not necessary.
- Change water every 4–5 days.
- Store away from direct heat and draughts.
- Remove any foliage in contact with water.

General Information:

- Long-lasting foliage suitable for using in both vase designs and floral foam.
- **Texture:** Bushy.
- **Leaf Shape:** Oval, slightly spoon shaped.
- **Would complement:** Round headed flowers such as carnations, roses and Dahlias.

 Brachyglottis (Dunedin Group) 'Sunshine' (Syn. *Senecio* 'Sunshine')

In Design and Wedding Work:

Dependable foliage which is very useful for funeral tributes either as filler or for foliage edging. Perfect for traditional arrangements, Brachyglottis will suit both pastel and more vibrant colour schemes. A perfect candidate for informal wedding work where it can be used in natural tied posies and table vases, but not a foliage for more contemporary designs. Suitable for corsages and boutonnieres.

For Students:

Family: Asteraceae.

Genus & Species: *Brachyglottis* sp.

Native to: New Zealand.

Trivia: 'Moria Read' is a variation of 'Sunshine' with cream and pale green leaves whose origins can be found at Liskeard, Cornwall.

27

Brunia

Common Name: **Silver Brunia**

Availability: June–March, peaks August–January.

Vase Life: 14–21 days.

Foliage Notes: A tall, elegant shrub with long slender branches carrying tiny flowers clustered tightly together to form small, rounded heads. Medium stem length.

Colour Range: Blue-green with silver-grey buds.

Conditioning:

- Ideal temperature range: 2–5°C (36–41°F).
- Re-cut stems, preferably with secateurs.
- Stand in clean water, flower food is not necessary.
- Change water every 4–5 days.
- Store away from direct heat and draughts.

General Information:

- Hardy and long-lasting, suitable for using in both vase designs and floral foam.
- **Texture:** Scaly/Rounded.
- **Leaf Shape:** Needle.
- **Would complement:** Flowers with interesting textures; Protea, Achillea or Anigozanthus.

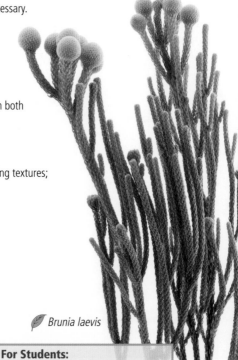

Brunia laevis

In Design and Wedding Work:

An interesting foliage, Brunia is often confined to making up 'safari' bunches, but it is much more versatile than that. Use it to add texture to arrangements, natural tied posies and funeral tributes; it is also great for Christmas designs where it will add a further dimension to door wreaths and garlands. Use in bridal designs where it will complement a white/green colour scheme. Suitable for wiring into boutonnières and corsages.

For Students:

Family: Bruniaceae.

Genus & Species: *Brunia* sp.

Native to: South Africa.

Trivia: Bruniaceae is an ancient family; fossil pollen that matches the modern Brunia has been discovered recently dating to over 65 million years ago.

Common Name: **Common box, Evergreen boxwood**

Availability: December–May, peaks December–April.

Vase Life: 10–14 days.

Foliage Notes: A slow growing, evergreen shrub with small, leathery leaves bearing insignificant pale yellow flowers followed by small green fruits. Medium stem length.

Colour Range: Dark green.

Conditioning:

- Ideal temperature range: 2–5°C (36–41°F).
- Re-cut stems at an angle, preferably with a knife or secateurs.
- Stand in clean, fresh water.
- Change water every 4–5 days and store away from direct heat and draughts.
- Don't overcrowd buckets; this can lead to leaf drop.

General Information:

- Woody stemmed, use secateurs and cut at an angle.
- Clean the stem of any foliage before inserting it into floral foam.
- **Texture:** Smooth.
- **Leaf shape:** Oval.
- **Would complement:** Small headed, shorter stemmed flowers.

In Design and Wedding Work:
Suitable for using in floral foam but its delicate leaves can get lost in large designs. Useful for funeral work, particularly for foliage edging and textured designs although cost must be taken into consideration. Box is often seen at weddings as ornamental topiary arranged in pairs outside church and venue entrances. Smaller versions of the same can be used as table designs. Box is also very useful for filling out garlanding and swags. **Foliage meaning:** Stoicism.

For Students:
Family: Buxaceae.
Genus & Species: *Buxus sempervirens*.
Native to: Europe, N. Africa, S. Asia.
Trivia: Box Hill in Surrey is named after its box population which is the largest area of box in England and one of the oldest areas of woodland in the UK.

Buxus sempervirens

29

Calathea

Common Name: **Zebra plant**

Availability: All year round.

Vase Life: 7–10 days.

Foliage Notes: Pronounced 'Ka-LA-thea'. A low growing tropical plant with attractive wavy edged leaves marked with distinctive, brightly coloured patches. Undersides of leaves are violet/purple. Short stem length.

Colour Range: Forest green with yellow, pink and brown markings.

Conditioning:

- Ideal temperature range: 12–15°C (54–59°F).
- Re-cut stems and stand in shallow, fresh water.
- Try to avoid water touching the bottom of the leaves.
- Change water every 2–3 days.
- Prefers a humid atmosphere, store away from direct heat and draughts.

General Information:

- Use in floral foam with care, as stems are quite soft.
- Can apply leaf shine.
- **Texture:** Smooth/Rippled.
- **Leaf Shape:** Lance.
- **Would complement:** Bright and vibrant short stemmed tropical flowers.

In Design and Wedding Work:
An ideal foliage for contemporary designs, Calathea can be manipulated, i.e. rolled and pinned, to provide a point of interest and enhance focal areas. For a bride with a modern tropical theme Calathea is a great choice, being both bold and striking. Add into limited style shower bouquets and use to create a colourful collar around tied posies. The leaves are generally a little too short for larger designs.

 Calathea zebrine

For Students:
Family: Marantaceae.
Genus & Species: *Calathea* sp.
Native to: Tropical Americas.
Trivia: Calathea leaves are multipurpose –in parts of Brazil they are used to wrap fish and the Nukak people of Columbia use them to make containers for their quivers.

Camellia

Availability: October–March.

Vase Life: 14–28 days.

Foliage Notes: A small ornamental evergreen tree grown primarily for its showy, waxy, rosette-shaped flowers. Medium stem length.

Colour Range: Glossy dark green.

Conditioning:

- Ideal temperature range: 2–5°C (36–41°F).
- Re-cut stems with secateurs.
- Stand in clean shallow water which should be topped up every few days.
- Flower food is not necessary.
- Store away from direct heat and draughts.

General Information:

- Use a damp cloth to clean leaves. Can use leaf shine sparingly.
- Woody stemmed, use secateurs.
- **Texture:** Smooth/Glossy.
- **Leaf Shape:** Elliptic.
- **Would complement:** Classic flowers such as peonies, roses and orchids.

x2 *Camellia japonica*

In Design and Wedding Work:

Camellia's attractive glossy foliage is suitable for both traditional and contemporary designs. In funeral work use it in textured arrangements and for foliage edging. In wedding work Camellia leaves can be pinned and layered, they also make excellent backing for buttonholes and corsages, although whole stems might be a bit unwieldy for bridal bouquets. Its dark green foliage would set off bolder flowers in large pedestal designs where it would provide sturdy and reliable support.

Foliage meaning: Perfected loveliness.

For Students:

Family: Theaceae.

Genus & Species: *Camellia japonica*.

Native to: East/south Asia.

Trivia: The most well-known member of the family is *Camellia sinensis*, from which tea is made.

31

Capsicum

Common Name: **Christmas pepper**

Availability: May–November.

Vase Life: 7–10 days.

Foliage Notes: A decorative plant grown for its attractive fruits rather than its foliage. Fruits are initially green, changing colour as they mature. Short stem length.

Colour Range: From bright yellow, orange and red to dark burgundy.

Conditioning:

- Ideal temperature range: 13–15°C (55–59°F).
- Re-cut stems, preferably with a knife.
- Stand in clean, shallow water.
- Change water every 3–4 days.
- Store away from direct heat and draughts which can cause fruits to drop.

General Information:

- Purely decorative, not to be consumed.
- Mist leaves gently every few days.
- Suitable for using in floral foam and vases, but try to avoid fruits touching wet surfaces.
- **Texture:** Smooth/Glossy.
- **Would complement:** Vivid, shorter stemmed flowers.

Capsicum annuum

In Design and Wedding Work:

Handled with care Capsicum are very effective in modern textured designs and decorative door wreaths, include into seasonal arrangements for a splash of vibrant colour. Ideal for autumn or Christmas weddings they will add a sense of fun to venue arrangements. If using in bridal work, handle with care as the fruits can snap easily. Avoid using them in designs for children in case they are tempted to eat them. Can be wired with care.

For Students:

Family: Solanaceae.

Genus & Species: *Capsicum annuum*.

Native to: The Americas.

Trivia: Capsicums have been cultivated for thousands of years, evidence of them has been found in pottery dating back to 3,000 BC.

Ceropegia

Availability: All year round.

Vase Life: 14–21 days.

Foliage Notes: Pronounced 'Sero-PEE-gea'. An evergreen trailing succulent with interesting tubular flowers. Popular in hanging baskets, it can grow up to 2–4m (6–13') under the right conditions.

Colour Range: Grey-green, purple, silver.

Conditioning:

- Ideal temperature range: 22–25°C (72–77°F).
- If buying a plant, cut as necessary when needed for designs.
- Keep the plant in a warm place, away from cold and draughts.
- Water only when dry, do not allow the plant to stand in water.
- Spray gently every few days.

General Information:

- Handle with care to avoid tangling the delicate stems.
- Long-lasting foliage suitable for using in both vase designs and floral foam.
- **Texture:** Smooth.
- **Leaf Shape:** Heart.
- **Would complement:** Small delicate flowers; Muscari, paperwhites, Hellebore.

In Design and Wedding Work:

A marvellously flexible and attractive plant, whose delicate trails can be wrapped, bound and wound into a variety of designs. Even though Ceropegia tends to be associated with more contemporary work, it can be used to great effect in more traditional arrangements, particularly with spring flowers. For weddings, use it to wind around the edges of tied posies or to trail elegantly from shower bouquets. Individual leaves can be glued into corsages or boutonnières.

 *Ceropegia linearis*
subsp. *woodii*

For Students:

Family: Apocynaceae.

Genus & Species: *Ceropegia linearis.*

Native to: South Africa.

Trivia: Ceropegia was discovered in 1881 in Nepal by the botanist John Medley Wood. He sent a sample to Kew Gardens in 1894 which was recorded in Curtis's Botanical Magazine in 1900.

Chaenomeles

Common Name: **Flowering quince, Japanese quince**

Availability: November–March.

Vase Life: 5–7 days.

Foliage Notes: Pronounced 'Sham-NOM-o-lees. A deciduous spiny shrub with attractive cup shaped flowers followed by quince-like fruits in summer. Medium stem length.

Colour Range: Bright green leaves, scarlet, pink or white flowers.

Conditioning:

- Ideal temperature range: 2–5°C (36–41°F).
- Woody stemmed so re-cut with secateurs.
- Stand in clean water and store away from direct heat and draughts.
- Change water every 2–3 days, re-cutting stems each time.

General Information:

- Handle carefully, gloves are recommended.
- Suitable for using in both vase designs and floral foam.
- Ensure containers are kept topped up with fresh water.
- **Texture:** Bushy.
- **Leaf Shape:** Oval.
- **Would complement:** Tall spring flowers; Viburnum, Forsythia or Syringa.

Chaenomeles x superba 'Crimson and Gold'

In Design and Wedding Work:

Chaenomeles will add height and structure to arrangements and can be used successfully in modern, linear designs. It will not be out of place either in more informal work where a natural 'garden' look is required. This is a foliage for the bride with a country theme, it can be used in reception arrangements but care should be taken where you place the designs as Chaenomeles has sharp spines, for this reason not suitable for hand-tied posies or wired work.

Foliage Meaning: Temptation.

For Students:

Family: Rosaceae.

Genus & Species: *Chaenomeles* sp.

Native to: Far East.

Trivia: Despite its common name Chaenomeles is not a true quince; these belong to the genus Cydonia.

Chamaecyparis

Common Name: **Lawson Cypress**

Availability: All year round.

Vase Life: 14–28 days.

Foliage Notes: Pronounced 'Sham-e-SEE-paris'. An evergreen conifer with flat, branched sprays that have small brown seed cones maturing in early autumn. Foliage is slightly aromatic. Medium stem length.

Colour Range: Dark to mid-green.

Conditioning:

- Ideal temperature range: 2–5°C (36–41°F).
- Can be left in bundles in polythene in a cold store room for up to two weeks.
- Store away from direct heat and draughts.
- Can store outside in winter.

General Information:

- Long-lasting foliage, suitable for designs in floral foam.
- **Texture:** Rough.
- **Would complement:** Traditional flowers; Chrysanthemums, carnations or Alstroemeria.

 *Chamaecyparis lawsoniana*

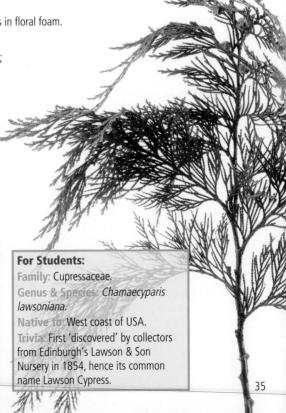

In Design and Wedding Work:

A foliage traditionally used for funeral tributes, although it's not as popular as it used to be. An inexpensive way to give bulk and outline to traditional arrangements. Not normally associated with wedding work as its stiff, flat foliage is out of step with today's bridal trends. That doesn't mean it has to be disregarded altogether though, for winter weddings its aromatic foliage can be used in pedestal designs and table arrangements where it will complement the traditional Christmas colours of red and gold.

For Students:

Family: Cupressaceae.

Genus & Species: *Chamaecyparis lawsoniana.*

Native to: West coast of USA.

Trivia: First 'discovered' by collectors from Edinburgh's Lawson & Son Nursery in 1854, hence its common name Lawson Cypress.

Choisya

Common Name: **Mexican orange blossom, Mock orange**

Availability: All year round.

Vase Life: 7–14 days.

Foliage Notes: Pronounced 'CHOY-see-ya'. An ornamental evergreen with aromatic leaves and fragrant, star-shaped flowers. *C. ternata* 'Sundance' is a bright yellow variety commonly seen in gardens. Medium stem length.

Colour Range: Mid-green to bright lime.

Conditioning:

- Ideal temperature range: 2–5°C (36–41°F).
- Re-cut stems, preferably with a knife.
- Stand in clean, fresh water with flower food.
- Store away from direct heat and draughts.
- Can apply leaf shine.

General Information:

- Choisya will last longer in vase designs than in floral foam.
- Ensure containers are kept topped up with water.
- **Texture:** Bushy.
- **Leaf shape:** Palmate.
- **Would complement:** Large headed, bold flowers in bright vibrant colours.

 Choisya ternata

In Design and Wedding Work:

This garden foliage is perfect for more natural styling. Ideal in traditional arrangements, it is a little too bushy for more contemporary work. For brides planning a wedding using traditional UK grown flowers then Choisya would be a foliage to consider. Add into pedestal arrangements in venues and churches and informal vase designs. Choisya will complement strong colours and flowers with simple lines. Unsuitable for wiring.

For Students:

Family: Rutaceae.

Genus & Species: *Choisya ternata*.

Native to: North America.

Trivia: The leaves have a fragrant scent when crushed, which is not dissimilar to the herb basil.

Cladonia

Common Name: **Reindeer moss, Reindeer lichen, Caribou moss**

Availability: All year round.

Vase Life: Indefinite.

Foliage Notes: Very slow growing soft lichen extensively branched with each tiny branch measuring approximately 1–1.5mm.

Colour Range: Off-white, grey, can be dyed a variety of colours.

Conditioning:

- Ideal temperature range: 2–5°C (36–41°F).
- Reindeer moss is typically sold in plastic containers which are ideal for long-term storage.
- Store in a dry place out of direct sunlight.
- Avoid storing in humid areas and direct heat sources.

General Information:

- Very long-lasting. If handled with care reindeer moss can be reused many times.
- Use wire pins to attach the moss to floral foam.
- If using in fresh designs dry the moss out before reusing to prevent mould.
- **Texture:** Spongy.

Cladonia stellaris

In Design and Wedding Work:

A soft, easy to handle lichen which will add texture to both fresh and dried arrangements. Reindeer moss isn't something that normally pops up in wedding flowers although it could potentially be used in winter arrangements to add texture to natural, vegetative designs. In modern bridal work, where the bride may be holding a sphere instead of a traditional handle, it could be used to cover mechanics and provide a soft area for her hand to rest.

For Students:

Family: Cladoniaceae.

Genus & Species: *Cladonia stellaris*.

Native to: Arctic & Northern regions.

Trivia: The Dena'ina, an Alaskan native people, eat reindeer moss crushed and boiled with berries or fish eggs to add flavour. Eat your heart out Delia.

Clematis

Common Name: **Traveller's joy, Old man's beard, Vase vine**

Availability: All year round, peaks September–January.

Vase Life: 10–14 days.

Foliage Notes: A popular climbing plant which scrambles easily over fences, trellises and trees. It produces a decorative fluffy seed head after flowering. Medium stem length.

Colour Range: Mid-green.

Conditioning:

- Ideal temperature range: 2–5°C (36–41°F).
- Re-cut stems, preferably with a knife.
- Stand in clean water with flower food.
- Change water every 2–3 days.
- Display away from direct heat and draughts.

General Information:

- Suitable for using in both vase designs and floral foam.
- Handle carefully, cutting, rather than pulling tendrils to separate stems.
- Texture: Fluffy.
- **Would complement:** Country garden flowers such as scabious, peony and roses.

 Clematis sp.

In Design and Wedding Work:

Use Clematis to trail out of, and soften the edges of large arrangements, it can also be wound around hand-tied bouquets to give a natural foliage collar. In wedding work, Clematis will tumble out of shower bouquets and give a soft, feminine look to hand-tied posies. It would be impressive used in large pedestal designs and would be an interesting and different foliage choice for garlanding and swaging. Its fluffy seed heads are great for adding texture.

Foliage meaning: Mental Beauty.

For Students:

Family: Ranunculaceae.

Genus & Species: *Clematis* sp.

Native to: Majority from China.

Trivia: Due to its great number of varieties, it is possible to have Clematis flowering in the garden for nearly every month of the year.

Cocculus

Common Name: **Laurel leaf Cocculus, Laurel leaf snail tree**

Availability: All year, peaks June–February.

Vase Life: 14–21 days.

Foliage Notes: Pronounced 'Kok-u-lus'. An elegant, medium sized tree which can grow up to a height of 20m (60ft). Very hardy, it is grown largely for its ornamental foliage. Tall stem length.

Colour Range: Dark glossy green.

Conditioning:

- Ideal temperature range: 2–5°C (36–41°F).
- Re-cut stems, preferably with a sharp knife.
- Stand in clean water, flower food is not necessary.
- Change water every 4–5 days.
- Store away from direct heat and draughts.

General Information:

- Poisonous – wash hands after use.
- Long-lasting foliage suitable for using in both vase designs and floral foam.
- **Texture:** Smooth.
- **Leaf Shape:** Lance.
- **Would complement:** Tall flowers such as lilies, Helianthus and Hippeastrum.

 x3 *Cocculus laurifolius*

In Design and Wedding Work:

A very popular foliage, the shiny green arching stems of Cocculus are extremely versatile. Their length makes them ideal for backing and adding shape and line to large traditional arrangements and funeral sprays. Individual leaves are strong enough to be manipulated and wired. In wedding work use Cocculus for swags and garlanding, pedestal designs, pew ends and top tables. Rolled leaves can be wired and added into boutonnières and corsages.

For Students:

Family: Menispermaceae.

Genus & Species: *Cocculus laurifolius.*

Native to: China & Japan.

Trivia: Hardy enough to tolerate freezing conditions, Cocculus branches are also pliable enough to be trained along trellis to become a glossy green screen in gardens.

Cocos

Common Name: **Coconut palm, Malayan coconut palm**

Availability: All year round.

Vase Life: 14–21 days.

Foliage Notes: A large palm tree, the only species in its genus, which can grow up to 30m (100'). The leaves remain entire the first year, before becoming increasingly more pinnate. Medium stem length.

Colour Range: Bright green.

Conditioning:

- Ideal temperature range: 12–15°C (54–59°F).
- Re-cut stems, preferably with a knife.
- Stand in clean, fresh, shallow water with flower food.
- Store in a warm environment away from direct heat and draughts.

General Information:

- Suitable for both vase designs and for floral foam.
- Can apply leaf shine.
- **Texture:** Glossy/Ribbed.
- **Leaf shape:** Lance maturing into pinnate.
- **Would complement:** Tall flowers – Strelitzia, Heliconia or Protea.

In Design and Wedding Work:

Use Cocos in structured design work to make the most of its distinctive shape. Leaves can also be rolled and pinned with care. For a tropical wedding its glossy leaves and bold shape would provide a strong backing for structural designs. Not something you would expect to see in a bridal bouquet, but perfect for impressive entrance arrangements and large table vases. If arranging in a vase, filling the vase with floral foam would provide a more secure anchor for this striking leaf.

 Cocos nucifera

For Students:

Family: Arecaceae.

Genus & Species: _Cocos nucifera_.

Native to: South Pacific.

Trivia: Known in the 16th century as cocoanut from Spanish 'cocos' meaning 'grinning face' a reference to the pattern formed by the three holes in the fruit.

Cordyline

Common Name: **Cordyline, Hawaiian palm, Ti palm, Good luck plant**

Availability: All year round.

Vase Life: 14–21 days.

Foliage Notes: An ornamental evergreen shrub with boldly coloured striped leaves. Popular as a centrepiece for containers and patio tubs. Medium stem length.

Colour Range: Dark to mid-green with brightly coloured margins.

Conditioning:

- Ideal temperature range: 12–15°C (54–59°F).
- Re-cut stems at an angle, preferably with a knife.
- Stand in clean, fresh water with flower food.
- Store away from direct heat and draughts in a warm environment.

General Information:

- Suitable for both vase designs and using in floral foam.
- Damaged or dying leaves can be peeled off the stem.
- **Texture:** Glossy.
- **Leaf shape:** Lance.
- **Would complement:** Anthurium, Liatris, Gerbera or Curcuma.

In Design and Wedding Work:

Cordyline will give line and a dash of bold colour in both modern and traditional designs, plus add depth to sprays on based tributes. The striking colours of Cordyline need to be carefully balanced against wedding colour schemes. 'Red Edge' for example, lends itself naturally to autumn or winter weddings where it will coordinate with cream, dark green and textured foliages and berries. Smaller leaves can be rolled and pinned for wired work.

 Cordyline fruticosa 'Red Edge'

For Students:

Family: Asparagaceae.

Genus & Species: *Cordyline* sp.

Native to: Pacific Ocean region.

Trivia: Hawaiians believe that the Ti plant brings good luck to their homes and plant them extensively around their houses.

Cornus

Common Name: **Dogwood**

Availability: August–March, peaks October–February.

Vase Life: 14–21 days.

Foliage Notes: A vigorous deciduous shrub with brightly coloured bare stems in winter. Popular with landscapers, red and yellow varieties are often contrasted next to each other. Tall stem length.

Colour Range: Bright red, green, yellow.

Conditioning:

● Ideal temperature range: 2–5°C (36–41°F).

● Re-cut stems, preferably with a sharp knife or secateurs.

● Stand in clean shallow water with flower food which will help to maintain its flexibility.

● Change water every 3–4 days.

● Store away from direct heat and draughts.

General Information:

● Suitable for both vase designs and floral foam, if using in foam keep container topped up.

● Cornus dies from the top down, withered stem ends can be cut off to improve appearance.

● **Texture:** Smooth.

● **Would complement:** Tall bold flowers.

x6
*Cornus
sericea*

x6
*Cornus
alba*

In Design and Wedding Work:

Use the erect stems of Cornus to create frameworks for modern, structured arrangements. Fresh cut Cornus is also flexible enough to bend and weave into design work. It will add height and definition to contemporary designs and would be particularly suitable in a more modern setting. Use full length for pedestal and tall vase designs, or, the other extreme, cut into small pieces which can then be wired into boutonnières and corsages to give them a contemporary edge.

For Students:

Family: Cornaceae.

Genus & Species: *Cornus* sp.

Native to: Eastern Asia.

Trivia: Cornus is very dense and is often used for making small items that require hard, resilient wood such as tool handles. P.S. How can you tell its dogwood? By its bark, of course.

Corylus

Common Name: **Contorted/Corkscrew hazel, Harry Lauder's walking stick**

Availability: August–April, peaks September–March.

Vase Life: 14–28 days in water, 3–6 months as a 'dried' twig.

Foliage Notes: An unusual tree with distinctive twisted branches. It has mustard yellow catkins in the spring followed by bright green leaves that are also misshapen. Medium/tall stem length.

Colour Range: Grey bark, yellow catkins.

Conditioning:

- Ideal temperature range: 2–5°C (36–41°F).
- Re-cut stems with secateurs and stand in clean, fresh water.
- Store away from direct heat to prevent stems drying out prematurely.
- Stems tangle easily, handle with care when separating.

General Information:

- Suitable for both vase designs and for floral foam.
- Can be stored in bundles out of water until needed.
- If using in floral foam anchor in securely to prevent it from moving.
- **Texture:** Smooth.
- **Would complement:** Bold, tall flowers; lilies, Eremurus or gladioli.

 ×3 *Corylus avellana* 'Contorta'

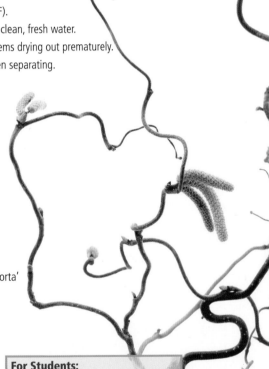

In Design and Wedding Work:

The twisted, contorted stems of this unusual tree give a wonderfully surreal look to designs. More suitable for contemporary, structured arrangements where the most can be made from its unique shape. The branches are strong enough to hang test tubes and water vials from. In wedding work, Corylus can be added into large pedestal designs and table vases where favours or decorations could be hung from its branches. Make sure that twigs are positioned so as to not snag on guest's outfits.

For Students:

Family: Betulaceae.

Genus & Species: *Corylus avellana.*

Native to: Europe & Western Asia.

Trivia: Harry Lauder (1870–1950) was a Scottish entertainer who at one point in his career was the highest paid performer in the world. One of his trademarks was a crooked walking stick.

43

Cotinus

Common Name: **Smoke bush, Smoke tree, Eurasian smoke tree**

Availability: May–November, peaks June–October.

Vase Life: 10–14 days.

Foliage Notes: A large deciduous shrub whose rich colours are popular in landscaping schemes where its distinctive coppery coloured foliage is unmistakable. Medium/tall stem length.

Colour Range: Wine red.

Conditioning:

- Ideal temperature range: 2–5°C (36–41°F).
- Re-cut stems, preferably with a sharp knife or secateurs.
- Remove foliage in contact with water, which should be changed every 3–4 days.
- Store away from direct heat to prevent leaf drop.
- Don't overcrowd buckets or containers.

General Information:

- Suitable for both vase designs and for floral foam.
- Woody stemmed, if using in floral foam keep containers topped up with water.
- **Texture:** Smooth.
- **Leaf shape:** Oval.
- **Would complement:** Flowers in autumnal shades of bronze, vibrant pink and orange.

Cotinus coggygria 'Royal Purple'
(Syn. *Rhus cotinus*)

In Design and Wedding Work:
Cotinus can be a useful filler in funeral designs and gift work. Add tall stems into large arrangements where its distinctive colour will add depth and contrast. Lovely for a late summer or autumn wedding where its rich colouring will provide a strong background to autumnal colour schemes. When adding into designs always make sure that any foliage in contact with wet surfaces is removed. Unsuitable for wiring.

For Students:
Family: Anacardiaceae.
Genus & Species: *Cotinus coggygria*.
Native to: Mediterranean & China.
Trivia: Grown in Britain since 1656, the name Cotinus comes from 'kotinus' the Greek for wild olive.

Cotinus

Availability: July–August.

Vase Life: 7–14 days.

Foliage Notes: This ornamental shrub produces small flowers borne in feathery inflorescences in summer which give the appearance of smoke, hence its common name. Medium/tall stem length.

Colour Range: Pink/red.

Conditioning:

- Ideal temperature range: 2–5°C (36–41°F).
- Re-cut stems, preferably with a sharp knife or secateurs.
- Remove foliage in contact with water, which should be changed every 3–4 days.
- Store away from direct heat.
- Don't overcrowd buckets or containers.

General Information:

- Suitable for both vase designs and for floral foam.
- Woody stemmed, if using in floral foam keep containers topped up with water.
- **Texture:** Feathery.
- **Leaf shape:** Oval.
- **Would complement:** Summer flowers in pastel colours; pinks, creams, pale blues.

 Cotinus coggygria 'Royal Purple' (Syn. *Rhus cotinus*)

In Design and Wedding Work:
Soft, feathery Cotinus has an almost magical appearance about it, perfect for creating summer designs that require something a little more ethereal. Most suitable for larger arrangements it would look stunning in marquee or outdoor weddings where the bride is looking for a very natural, garden feel. Be careful when handling as the delicate flowers crush and stick together easily. For this reason, avoid spraying with water. Can be wired into designs with care.

For Students:
Family: Anacardiaceae.
Genus & Species: *Cotinus coggygria*.
Native to: Mediterranean & China.
Trivia: One of the oldest specimens of Cotinus can be found at the National Trust's garden at Hidcote Manor in Gloucestershire.

45

Crocosmia

Common Name: **Montbretia**

Availability: July–October.

Vase Life: 7–14 days.

Foliage Notes: An autumn flower which brightens up gardens with its vibrant orange hues. The seed heads from the mature flowers are a great addition to seasonal designs. Medium stem length.

Colour Range: Dark green – chestnut brown.

Conditioning:

- Ideal temperature range: 2–5°C (41–46°F).
- Re-cut stems, preferably with a knife.
- Stand in clean water with flower food.
- Change water every 4–5 days, re-cutting stems each time.
- Handle with care, as stems can become easily tangled.

General Information:

- Suitable for using in both vase designs and floral foam.
- The sword-like leaves of Crocosmia are not as robust as the stems and seed head.
- **Texture:** Beaded.
- **Leaf Shape:** Linear.
- **Would complement:** Autumnal flowers; Dahlia, Celosia and Chrysanthemum.

In Design and Wedding Work:
Use Crocosmia in more limited, contemporary designs to show off its arching shape and attractive seed heads. It will also add texture and line to loose, garden style tributes. Crocosmia would be a perfect addition to an autumn wedding, not only is it a traditional garden flower, suiting brides looking for a more natural style, but its delicate seed heads will add delightful texture to tied posies and vase designs. Suitable for wiring into corsages and boutonnières.

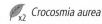 *Crocosmia aurea*

For Students:
Family: Iridaceae.
Genus & Species: *Crocosmia* sp.
Native to: South Africa.
Trivia: A hardy perennial, there are over 400 cultivars of Crocosmia worldwide. In some parts of the world it is regarded as an invasive species.

Common Name: **Gourd, Pumpkin, Squash**

Availability: August–October.

Vase Life: 10–15 days.

Foliage Notes: One of the seasonal pleasures of autumn, these colourful gourds vary in size from tiny fruits to huge pumpkins ready to be carved for Halloween.

Colour Range: Green, yellow, orange, plain, bicoloured and striped.

Conditioning:

- Ideal temperature range: 2–5°C (36–41°F).
- Store in cool conditions until needed to extend its shelf life.
- Do not store or stand gourds in damp or wet areas.
- Display away from direct heat.

General Information:

- Gourds grown for commercial decoration shouldn't be consumed.
- Delivered wholesale in crates or available to buy individually.
- **Texture:** Smooth/Ribbed.
- **Would complement:** Autumnal flowers and foliage, textured materials.

Cucurbita sp.

In Design and Wedding Work:

A staple of autumn designs, gourds are often an integral part of arrangements in floral foam, although care should be taken when positioning them as they can be top heavy. Use garden canes to anchor them into designs, try to avoid them touching damp surfaces as this will cause them to rot. Use gourds creatively in wedding work by scattering them on tables, carving faces and adding candles or flowers for spooky Halloween table arrangements.

For Students:

Family: Cucurbitaceae.

Genus & Species: *Cucurbita* sp.

Native to: South America.

Trivia: Squash comes from the Native American word 'askutasquash', meaning 'eaten raw'. It was first brought to Europe by Spanish adventurers in the 16th century.

47

Cycas

Common Name: **Sago palm**

Availability: October–July, peaks October–March.

Vase Life: 14–28 days.

Foliage Notes: A deciduous palm, popular as a landscaping plant in warm climates. Very slow growing, it can take up to 100 years for it to reach 6m (20') in height. Medium stem length.

Colour Range: Dark green.

Conditioning:

- Ideal temperature range: 12–15°C (54–59°F).
- Re-cut stems and stand in clean, shallow water.
- Don't overcrowd containers and handle with care.
- Can use leaf shine.
- Store away from direct heat and draughts.

General Information:

- Long-lasting foliage suitable for using in both vase designs and floral foam.
- Trim off the bottom leaves from the stem before placing in floral foam.
- Brown tips can be trimmed carefully with scissors.
- **Texture:** Ribbed.
- **Leaf Shape:** Lance.
- **Would complement:** Tropical flowers; Strelitzia, Heliconia or Anthurium.

In Design and Wedding Work:

Cycas gives a dramatic outline to contemporary designs and funeral sprays; although it's not recommended for hand-tied designs as the foliage is very spiky. A choice foliage to use in modern wedding venues where the bride has chosen a contemporary or tropical theme. Cycas can be added into in arrangements in floral foam, but when using in public areas or on reception tables, make sure that the prickly foliage won't be in contact with visitors or guests.

 Cycas revoluta

For Students:

Family: Cycadaceae.

Genus & Species: *Cycas revoluta*.

Native to: Southern Japan.

Trivia: A member of an ancient group of plants, a large number of which are threatened with extinction, Cycas are protected under the CITES convention.

Cyclamen

Availability: October–April.

Vase Life: 7–10 days.

Foliage Notes: Sold as a flowering houseplant (although commercially cut Cyclamen is available from The Netherlands) the distinctive leaves are also used in floral designs. Short stem length.

Colour Range: Dark green with silvery markings.

Conditioning:

- Ideal temperature range: 2–5°C (36–41°F).
- If using a plant, carefully cut stems with scissors.
- Stand in clean, shallow water in a bowl or small vase.
- Ensure leaves are not touching the water.
- Store away from direct heat and draughts.

General Information:

- The fleshy stems of Cyclamen can be wired with care for extra support and control.
- **Texture:** Smooth/Patterned.
- **Leaf Shape:** Rounded.
- **Would complement:** Delicate spring flowers; snowdrops, Muscari or Narcissus.

 Cyclamen persicum

In Design and Wedding Work:
Cyclamen leaves are too short for using in anything but the tiniest of vase designs, but its delicate patterning makes it attractive foliage to add into sprays on funeral tributes. The ivy-like leaves of Cyclamen can be wired into buttonholes, corsages and boutonnières. Their stems are too short for tied posies, but can be added into bouquets made in floral foam holders. They could also be attached onto wired frameworks or popped into glass test tubes.

Flower Meaning: Diffidence.

For Students:
Family: Primulaceae.

Genus & Species: *Cyclamen* sp.

Native to: Mediterranean, N. Africa.

Trivia: The Cyclamen species is so diverse it is possible to have a flowering plant for every month of the year.

49

Cyperus

Common Name: **Umbrella sedge, Umbrella grass**

Availability: All year round.

Vase Life: 5–7 days.

Foliage Notes: Aquatic flowering plants, popularly grown as ornamental pond plants but also commonly available as houseplants. Medium stem length.

Colour Range: Dark green.

Conditioning:

- Ideal temperature range: 12–15°C (54–59°F).
- Re-cut stems, preferably with scissors and stand in deep, clean water with flower food.
- Change water every 2–3 days and keep containers topped up.
- Store away from direct heat and draughts.

Cyperus papyrus

General Information:

- Dries out extremely easily, mist daily and don't leave out of water for any length of time.
- Suitable for using in both vase designs and floral foam.
- **Texture:** Spiky.
- **Leaf Shape:** Strap.
- **Would complement:** Striking, bold flowers; Gerbera,Heliconia, Liatris.

In Design and Wedding Work:
Not foliage that you would normally associate with traditional designs, its unusual and interesting shape is perfect for more exciting, contemporary work. Their long, straight, leafless stems will add strong vertical lines and direction to structured hand-ties and arrangements. Group and step them for maximum effect. Be wary of using Cyperus in contract work as they dry out quickly in warm conditions. *C. papyrus* can be dried however – air dry or use glycerine to keep its glossy looks.

 Cyperus alternifolius

For Students:

Family: Cyperaceae.

Genus & Species: *Cyperus* sp.

Native to: Subtropical Africa.

Trivia: *C. papyrus* has many uses outside of flower arranging. Its buoyant stems are light enough to be made into boats, and it was famously a source of paper for the Ancient Egyptians.

Danae

Common Name: **Soft ruscus, Alexandrian laurel, Poet's laurel**

Availability: All year round.

Vase Life: 14–21 days.

Foliage Notes: An elegant evergreen with tall, arching stems. Male and female flowers are borne on the same plant, which produces orange-red berries in autumn. Medium/tall stem length.

Colour Range: Dark glossy green.

Conditioning:

- Ideal temperature range: 2–5°C (36–41°F).
- Re-cut stems, preferably with a sharp knife.
- Remove foliage in contact with water, which should be changed every 3–4 days.
- Store away from direct heat and draughts.
- Don't overcrowd buckets or containers.

General Information:

- Suitable for both vase designs and for arrangements in floral foam.
- **Texture:** Glossy.
- **Leaf shape:** Lance.
- **Would complement:** Tall flowers; Hippeastrum, Delphinium, lilies or Chrysanthemum.

x5 *Danae racemosa*

In Design and Wedding Work:

Soft ruscus is perfect for adding elegant line and height to large arrangements; it can also be cut into small pieces and used as edging for funeral tributes. A popular foliage for weddings, where it can be included in traditional shower bouquets to give softness and movement or used to edge hand-tied posies. The lengthy stems are great for garlanding; they are also strong enough for attaching flowers onto. It can be used in wired work although it may be a little bit fussy for small, delicate designs.

For Students:

Family: Asparagaceae.

Genus & Species: *Danae racemosa.*

Native to: Asia Minor.

Trivia: The glossy leaves are in fact flattened stems, designed to store water in dry conditions, a direct result of the hot, dry countries *D. racemosa* is native to.

51

Diplocyclos

Common Name: **Striped cucumber, Lollypop climber**

Availability: September–March.

Vase Life: 5–7 days.

Foliage Notes: Pronounced 'dip-low-SY-clos'. A slender climbing plant which bears unusual grape sized striped fruits in the autumn. Long stem length.

Colour Range: Light green with white stripes, fruit turns red as it matures.

Conditioning:

- Ideal temperature range: 8–10°C (46–50°F).
- Re-cut stem ends, preferably with a knife.
- Display in clean, shallow water ensuring that the fruits are kept dry.
- Change water every 2–3 days.

General Information:

- Needs good air circulation to prevent the fruits from going mouldy.
- Avoid spraying fruits, leaf shine is not necessary.
- **Texture:** Smooth.
- **Would complement:** Textured flowers and foliage to show off its unusual shape.

Diplocyclos palamatus

In Design and Wedding Work:

An attractive and unusual decorative fruit, particularly suitable for autumn designs. Try wrapping Diplocyclos around the inside of glass bowls for an unusual centrepiece or weaving it though a textured funeral tribute. It can be combined into wedding designs, but it does need space to be appreciated – not something to add to a large showy arrangement - but it would make an interesting addition to more structured, limited designs. The fruit is poisonous, so be careful using it where small children are involved.

For Students:

Family: Cucurbitaceae.

Genus & Species: *Diplocyclos palmatus.*

Native to: Australasia.

Trivia: A member of the family that includes cucumbers and gourds, Diplocyclos has become a threat to native vegetation in some parts of the world.

Dracaena

Common Name: **Lucky bamboo**

Availability: All year round.

Vase Life: 14–28 days.

Foliage Notes: Pronounced 'Dra-SCENE-a'. A distinctive and recognisable cane-like appearance with a corkscrew stem. Despite its common name, it is not related to bamboo. Medium/tall stem length.

Colour Range: Bright green.

Conditioning:

- Ideal temperature range: 12–15°C (54–59°F).
- Re-cut stems, preferably with a sharp knife or secateurs.
- Stand in shallow, fresh water, which should be changed every 3–4 days.
- Store away from direct heat and draughts.
- Handle with care as stems can tangle easily.

General Information:

- Suitable for both vase designs and floral foam.
- If left standing in water it will grow shoots and roots.
- Brown ends can be cut off, although this will gradually shorten the stem.
- **Texture:** Ribbed.
- **Would complement:** Sculptural flowers; Anthurium, Spathiphyllum or Heliconia.

x2 *Dracaena sanderiana*

In Design and Wedding Work:

To make the most of its unusual shape, Lucky Bamboo needs space; modern design work is its natural home. It is easier to control in floral foam, as it has a mind of its own with a tendency to 'turn' in hand-tied designs. Tall flowers can be threaded through its curls. A very specific foliage to use for weddings, it can look very effective in large, modern pedestal designs in contemporary settings, or would certainly provide a talking point if added into table arrangements.

For Students:

Family: Dracaenaceae.

Genus & Species: *Dracaena sanderiana.*

Native to: Cameroon & West Africa.

Trivia: Lucky bamboo's twisted shape is artificially made by rotating the stem in relation to gravity and light. It has strong associations with feng shui.

53

Dracaena

Common Name: **Ribbon plant**

Availability: All year round.

Vase Life: 14–28 days.

Foliage Notes: Known as ribbon plant for it leaf markings, this attractive foliage grows as an understory plant in rain forests. Medium stem length.

Colour Range: Light green with creamy margins.

Conditioning:

- Ideal temperature range: 12–15°C (54–59°F).
- Re-cut stems, preferably with a sharp knife or secateurs.
- Stand in fresh water which should be changed every 3–4 days.
- Store away from direct heat and draughts.
- Spray occasionally to maintain humidity.

General Information:

- Suitable for both vase designs and floral foam.
- Brown tips can be carefully trimmed off.
- **Texture:** Smooth.
- **Leaf shape:** Lance.
- **Would complement:** Bright flowers; Liatris, Anthurium or Longiflorum lily.

In Design and Wedding Work:

Attractive foliage which will enhance both hand-tied designs and arrangements. Its cream edged leaves and light green colouring will complement nearly all colour schemes; group it in modern designs for maximum impact. Individual leaves can be rolled and added into funeral sprays on based tributes. Lovely and light for weddings, it is versatile enough to be included in large venue designs or its attractive leaves can be wired as part of a boutonnière or corsage.

 Dracaena sanderiana

For Students:

Family: Dracaenaceae.

Genus & Species: *Dracaena sanderiana*.

Native to: Cameroon & West Africa.

Trivia: The genus is named after the German born orchid grower and businessman Henry Frederick Conrad Sander.

Dracaena

Availability: All year round.

Vase Life: 14–28 days.

Foliage Notes: An ornamental tropical foliage, shrub-like in appearance with broad, thin leaves boldly marked with irregular splashes. Medium stem length.

Colour Range: Light green with creamy markings.

Conditioning:

- Ideal temperature range: 12–15°C (54–59°F).
- Re-cut stems, preferably with a sharp knife or secateurs.
- Stand in fresh water, which should be changed every 3–4 days.
- Store away from direct heat and draughts.
- Spray occasionally to maintain humidity.

General Information:

- Suitable for both vase designs and for floral foam.
- **Texture:** Smooth.
- **Leaf shape:** Oval.
- **Would complement:** Vibrant flowers such as Gerbera, Calendula or shamrock blooms.

Dracaena surculosa cv. 'Florida Beauty'

In Design and Wedding Work:

Due to its bold colouring and markings, gold dust Dracaena will only work with certain colour combinations. Best seen in arrangements where its unusual pattern can be appreciated rather than in traditional hand-tied designs where it could get a little lost. Great foliage for tropical designs and it would work well with an autumn wedding if the bride is looking for typical seasonal shades of reds, gold and green.

For Students:

Family: Dracaenaceae.

Genus & Species: *Dracaena surculosa*.

Native to: Tropical West Africa.

Trivia: *Dracaena surculosa* can be grown as a houseplant, it needs a sunny spot, out of direct sunlight and moist, not over wet, compost.

Elaeagnus

Common Name: **Silverberry, Oleaster**

Availability: September–March.

Vase Life: 14–21 days.

Foliage Notes: Pronounced 'el-e-AG-nus'. A spiny, woody shrub with distinctively marked leaves and small fragrant flowers which mature into small fruits. Medium/tall stem length.

Colour Range: Dark to mid-green with sulphur yellow markings.

Conditioning:

- Ideal temperature range: 2–5°C (36–41°F).
- Re-cut stems, preferably with a sharp knife or secateurs.
- Stand in shallow, fresh water which should be changed every 3–4 days.
- Store away from direct heat and draughts.
- Remove any foliage in contact with water.

General Information:

- Handle with care as the stems have sharp spines.
- Prone to leaf drop as it matures.
- Due to its somewhat unwieldy shape, more suitable for using in floral foam than in vases.
- **Texture:** Smooth.
- **Leaf shape:** Ovate.
- **Would complement:** Natural garden flowers in yellow/green/white colour schemes.

Elaeagnus pungens

In Design and Wedding Work:

Elaeagnus leaves are tough enough to be overlapped and pinned to cover floral foam; it is also excellent for foliage edging and as filler for funeral sprays. Elaeagnus is not suitable for hand-tied work because of its woody spines unless you have the patience to carefully cut them off! It is very useful for filling out large pedestal arrangements in churches and venues — as long as the colour scheme fits. Individual leaves can be wired for buttonholes and boutonnières.

For Students:

Family: Elaeagnaceae.

Genus & Species: *Elaeagnus pungens.*

Native to: Asia.

Trivia: The thorny spines and woody stems of Elaeagnus make them ideal nesting habitats for birds.

Common Name: **Thatching reed**

Availability: All year, peaks June–November.

Vase Life: 7–14 days.

Foliage Notes: An ornamental reed with a tufty appearance which occurs naturally in marshes. In gardens it will thrive in moist soil alongside ponds. Medium stem length.

Colour Range: Light green and chocolate brown.

Conditioning:

- Ideal temperature range: 2–5°C (36–41°F).
- Re-cut stems with sharp scissors.
- Stand in clean water, flower food is not necessary.
- Change water every 4–5 days.
- Store away from direct heat and draughts in a spot with good air circulation.

General Information:

- Suitable for using in both vase designs and floral foam.
- High humidity is important to stop it from dropping.
- **Texture:** Rough.
- **Would complement:** Rich autumnal flowers; Dahlia, Crocosmia, Celosia or Hypericum.

In Design and Wedding Work:

A lovely textured reed which will add line and elegance to designs. Group in threes or fives to give maximum impact. Most suitable for summer and autumn designs where it will bring a welcome touch of seasonality and movement. Elegia would be excellent foliage for natural tied posies or even more formal shower bouquets. Not suitable for wiring as the tiny brown flowers can shed if handled too often.

Elegia tectorum

For Students:

Family: Restionaceae.

Genus & Species: *Elegia tectorum.*

Native to: South Africa.

Trivia: The Latin word tectorum means 'on roofs', referring to the fact that the reed has been used for thatching houses.

57

Equisetum

Common Name: **Horsetail, Scouring rush, Snake grass**

Availability: All year round.

Vase Life: 7–14 days.

Foliage Notes: A rush-like perennial with a hollow stem found growing in moist forests, along the banks of streams and in swamps and fens. Medium stem length.

Colour Range: Dark green with black banding.

Conditioning:

- Ideal temperature range: 2–5°C (36–41°F).
- Re-cut stems with scissors, leaving a flat edge.
- Stand in shallow, fresh water, change every 3–4 days.
- Store away from direct heat and draughts.
- If bunched in elastic bands, remove them as they can mark stems.

General Information:

- Equisetum will yellow as it ages, trim these sections off with scissors.
- If using in floral foam make a small hole first, this will help to push stems into the foam.
- Texture: Ridged.
- Would complement: Smaller tropical flowers; Anthurium, orchid or Eucharis lily.

In Design and Wedding Work:
Equisetum is very effective in modern, structured designs both hand-tied or in floral foam. Use vertically in groups for impact or by inserting a wire, bend into asymmetrical/symmetrical shapes. If planning a modern, contemporary wedding then Equisetum is useful foliage as it can be manipulated to create a framework. Cut into small pieces to add an unusual designer touch to boutonnières, buttonholes and corsages.

 Equisetum hyemale

For Students:
Family: Equisetaceae.
Genus & Species: *Equisetum hyemale.*
Native to: Eurasia, N. America.
Trivia: Equisetum's rough bristles were once used to scour pots; dried and ground it can also be used as a polishing material.

Eucalyptus

Common Name: **Gum tree, Silver dollar tree, Argyle apple**

Availability: All year round.

Vase Life: 10–14 days.

Foliage Notes: A fast growing tree with soft circular leaves becoming more oval as they mature. A primary food for Koala bears in Australia, its flowers are also very popular with bees. Medium stem length.

Colour Range: Silvery-grey.

Conditioning:

- Ideal temperature range: 2–5°C (36–41°F).
- Re-cut stems, preferably with a knife.
- Change water every 3–4 days and store away from direct heat and draughts.
- Requires high humidity to stop it from drying out.
- Remove all foliage in contact with water.

General Information:

- Reliable foliage suitable for using in both vase designs and floral foam.
- Larger leaves can crease easily, handle with care.
- **Texture:** Smooth.
- **Leaf Shape:** Round.
- **Would complement:** Bold flowers in rich shades; purples, blues and cerise pinks.

Eucalyptus cinerea

In Design and Wedding Work:
Use in traditional hand-tied designs to add volume and a subtle background colour which will help to enhance flowers. Very good for large, showy arrangements where its slightly trailing habit can be used to its best advantage. When cut into smaller sections, the large, almost flat leaves come in very handy to hide floral foam in smaller designs. *E. cinerea* can be used in wedding work in more natural, informal designs. Small sections can also be wired, but beware of the sticky sap.

For Students:
Family: Myrtaceae.
Genus & Species: *Eucalyptus cinerea*.
Native to: Australia.
Trivia: 'Argyle apple' derives from County Argyle in New South Wales, named by Governor Macquarie in the early nineteenth century after his native county in Scotland.

Eucalyptus

Common Name: Small-leafed gum

Availability: September–May.

Vase Life: 7–10 days.

Foliage Notes: A very fast growing evergreen with slightly aromatic grey-green foliage. It has insignificant clusters of small white, yellow or red flowers. Medium stem length.

Colour Range: Grey-green.

Conditioning:

- Ideal temperature range: 2–5°C (36–41°F).
- Re-cut stems, preferably with a knife.
- Change water every 3–4 days and store away from direct heat and draughts.
- Requires high humidity to prevent it from drying out.
- Remove all foliage in contact with water.

General Information:

- Reliable foliage suitable for using in both vase designs and floral foam.
- Do not overcrowd buckets and avoid misting.
- Beware of sticky sap.
- **Texture:** Bushy.
- **Leaf Shape:** Elliptic.
- **Would complement:** Large, unfussy flowers.

 x3 *Eucalyptus parvifolia*

In Design and Wedding Work:

Very useful for filling out large arrangements and for foliage edging funeral tributes, but not attractive enough to be a focal foliage. Also a little too untidy for hand-tied designs this is not a foliage to take centre stage in wedding work, but is very handy for large pedestal arrangements in churches or venues where it can be used as an inexpensive filler. Its delicate grey-green leaves would complement summery colour schemes of purples, pinks and blues. Not suitable for wiring work or contemporary bridal designs.

For Students:

Family: Myrtaceae.

Genus & Species: *Eucalyptus parvifolia*.

Native to: Majority to Australia.

Trivia: There are over 700 species of Eucalyptus, only 15 of which occur outside of Australia. The most northerly species is found in the Philippines.

60

Eucalyptus

Common Name: **Baby blue, Silver-leaved mountain gum**

Availability: September–May.

Vase Life: 7–14 days.

Foliage Notes: A slow growing, compact evergreen tree which bears clusters of small creamy white flowers in summer. The aromatic foliage has a silvery white blush. Medium stem length.

Colour Range: Blue-green.

Conditioning:

- Ideal temperature range: 2–5°C (36–41°F).
- Re-cut stems, preferably with a knife.
- Do not overcrowd buckets and avoid misting as this can rot the foliage.
- Change water every 3–4 days.
- Store away from direct heat and draughts.

General Information:

- Has a sticky sap which can mark clothing and fingers.
- Use scissors or a knife to strip stems.
- **Texture:** Smooth.
- **Leaf Shape:** Round.
- **Would complement:** Focal flowers; lilies, Gerbera, carnations or roses.

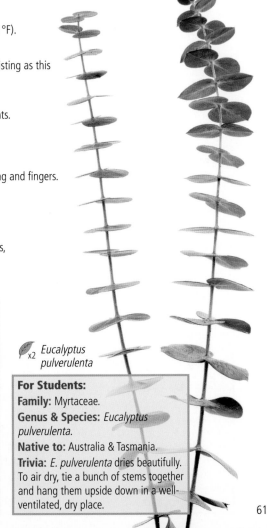

×2 *Eucalyptus pulverulenta*

In Design and Wedding Work:

Sculptural foliage which will add an interesting contrast to both vases and floral foam. Wonderful for festive designs and Christmas weddings, as not only does it give off a subtle, spicy scent but it coordinates beautifully with seasonal foliages and flowers. In December it can be bought dipped in gold or silver paint. Suitable for shower bouquets and tied posies, baby blue will give an extra dimension to buttonholes, corsages and boutonnières, but use with care, the sticky sap can make taping stems a tricky business.

For Students:

Family: Myrtaceae.

Genus & Species: *Eucalyptus pulverulenta*.

Native to: Australia & Tasmania.

Trivia: *E. pulverulenta* dries beautifully. To air dry, tie a bunch of stems together and hang them upside down in a well-ventilated, dry place.

Euonymus

Common Name: **Spindle tree**

Availability: All year round.

Vase Life: 14–21 days.

Foliage Notes: Pronounced 'U-on-e-mus'. A popular evergreen garden shrub with decorative bright foliage. Small, insignificant flowers are followed by colourful fruits in the autumn. Medium stem length.

Colour Range: Dark to light green with yellow/white variegation.

Conditioning:

- Ideal temperature range: 2–5°C (36–41°F).
- Re-cut stems, preferably with a knife.
- Stand in clean water, flower food is not necessary.
- Change water every 4–5 days and store away from direct heat and draughts.
- Don't overcrowd containers, as this can cause early leaf drop.

General Information:

- Long-lasting foliage suitable for using in both vase designs and floral foam.
- Not generally available as a commercial cut foliage.
- **Texture:** Bushy.
- **Leaf Shape:** Oval.
- **Would complement:** Traditional garden flowers.

 Euonymus fortunei

In Design and Wedding Work:

Very useful for loose funeral work, sprays and foliage edging, Euonymus is informal foliage which would work well in natural tied posies and simple vase designs. Its strong colours would suit wedding schemes with possibly more of an autumnal feel – it would work very well with limes, rich reds and berries such as Hypericum. Mature leaves can be wired into corsages, circlets and boutonnières.

Foliage Meaning: Your charms are engraved on my heart.

For Students:

Family: Celastraceae.

Genus & Species: *Euonymus* sp.

Native to: Asia.

Trivia: Euonymus is a great subject for topiary. It's a good alternative to box as it is faster growing and will withstand heavy pruning.

Euphorbia

Common Name: **Martin's spurge**

Availability: March–June.

Vase Life: 7–10 days.

Foliage Notes: Dwarf evergreen shrub with tiny, attractive flowers which grow in the form of leafy rosettes; its handsome foliage is excellent for interest in the garden. Medium stem length.

Colour Range: Lime green with purple and yellow tinged flowers.

Conditioning:

- Ideal temperature range: 8–12°C (46–54°F).
- Re-cut stems with scissors, washing hands afterwards.
- Sensitive to temperature fluctuations and ethylene gas.
- Change water every 2–3 days.
- Store away from direct heat and draughts.

General Information:

- Euphorbia's milky sap is toxic and an irritant, handle with care.
- Suitable for using in both vase designs and floral foam.
- **Texture:** Bushy.
- **Leaf Shape:** Elliptic/Ovate.
- **Would complement:** Spring flowers in jewel colours.

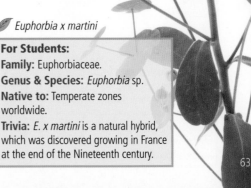

Euphorbia x martini

In Design and Wedding Work:
Striking foliage which will stand out wherever it is used, its bright lime acting as a foil to similarly vividly coloured flowers. To limit latex seepage from stems cut underwater and use flower food, also wash hands after use. As it is an irritant, it's better to avoid using it in hand-tied work, and for the same reason it's unsuitable for wiring. To see Euphorbia at its best, add it into large, showy arrangements with vibrant, bright flowers.

For Students:
Family: Euphorbiaceae.
Genus & Species: *Euphorbia* sp.
Native to: Temperate zones worldwide.
Trivia: *E. x martini* is a natural hybrid, which was discovered growing in France at the end of the Nineteenth century.

63

Fatsia

Common Name: **Aralia, Japanese aralia**

Availability: All year round.

Vase Life: 10–14 days.

Foliage Notes: A tough, evergreen shrub with large, bold leaves. It produces of creamy white flowers followed by purple-black berries in autumn. Short stem length.

Colour Range: Dark green.

Conditioning:

- Ideal temperature range: 2–5°C (36–41°F).
- Re-cut stems before putting into suitably sized containers.
- Stand in clean, shallow water which should be changed every 4–5 days.
- Store away from direct heat and draughts.
- Don't overcrowd buckets or let leaves touch the water.

General Information:

- Long-lasting foliage suitable for using in both vase designs and floral foam.
- Fatsia's bold shape lends itself to more contemporary, structured work.
- **Texture:** Smooth.
- **Leaf Shape:** Palmate.
- **Would complement:** Tropical or large headed flowers.

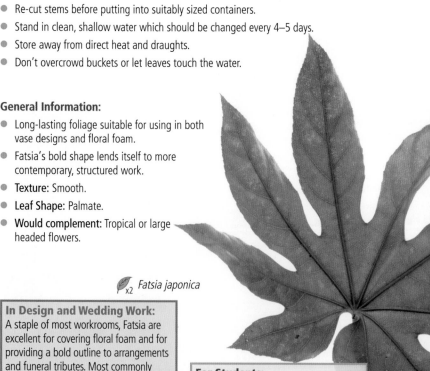

 Fatsia japonica

In Design and Wedding Work:

A staple of most workrooms, Fatsia are excellent for covering floral foam and for providing a bold outline to arrangements and funeral tributes. Most commonly used in wedding work for edging tied posies, although its solid shape means that it needs to be used with care else it can overpower more delicate designs. A useful foliage to enhance focal areas of pedestal arrangements, it can also be used to provide a collar to complete hand-tieds and vase designs.

For Students:

Family: Araliaceae.

Genus & Species: *Fatsia japonica*.

Native to: Eastern Asia.

Trivia: Fatsia was introduced into the UK in the early part of the 19th Century where it quickly became established in Victorian landscaping.

Galax

Availability: All year round.

Vase Life: 10–21 days.

Foliage Notes: An evergreen herbaceous plant whose leaves grow in a rosette shape at the base of its stem. They turn a reddish brown in autumn months. Short stem length.

Colour Range: Mossy green.

Conditioning:

- Ideal temperature range: 2–5°C (36–41°F).
- Galax is usually delivered in sealed plastic bags and should be unpacked on arrival.
- Re-cut stems with scissors and stand in fresh water in shallow containers.
- Change water every 4–5 days and store away from direct heat and draughts.
- Undo the bundles of leaves if not being used straight away.

General Information:

- Mist occasionally and try to keep leaves out of contact with water.
- **Texture:** Smooth.
- **Leaf Shape:** Reniform.
- **Would complement:** Short stemmed flowers; Hellebore, Fritillaria, Paphiopedilum.

Galax urceolata

In Design and Wedding Work:

Galax leaves are very versatile in arrangements and last well in floral foam. A little too small for all but the most petite of vase designs and would be completely lost in tied posies, but are very handy for filling in centres, as well as backing formal bridal bouquets in holders. Rolled leaves add a modern slant to buttonholes, boutonnières and corsages. Contemporary ball style bouquets can be partially covered in Galax leaves to create a smooth area for the brides hand to rest.

For Students:

Family: Diapensiaceae.

Genus & Species: *Galax urceolata*.

Native to: S/E USA.

Trivia: Galax is found mainly in the Appalachian Mountains growing up to altitudes of 500m (1500'). The city of Galax in Virginia is named after the plant.

Garrya

Common Name: **Silk tassel bush**

Availability: All year round.

Vase Life: 14–21 days.

Foliage Notes: An ornamental evergreen shrub with wavy edged leaves that have a woolly surface underneath. Attractive catkins appear in late winter and early spring. Medium stem length.

Colour Range: Dark green with silvery-green catkins.

Conditioning:

- Ideal temperature range: 2–5°C (36–41°F).
- Re-cut stems, preferably with secateurs.
- Stand in clean water, flower food is not necessary.
- Change water every 4–5 days.
- Store away from direct heat and draughts.

General Information:

- The catkins on male plants are the most impressive.
- Long-lasting foliage suitable for using in both vase designs and floral foam.
- **Texture:** Bushy.
- **Leaf Shape:** Oval.
- **Would complement:** Garden grown and spring flowers.

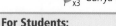 *Garrya elliptica*

In Design and Wedding Work:
To use Garrya at its most interesting, select it when its catkins are showing in winter and spring. Suitable for large pedestal arrangements or informal vase designs and great for adding texture and interest, although the catkins won't be seen to their best advantage in hand-tied arrangements. The leaves are sturdy enough to be rolled and wired into buttonholes and corsages. Lovely foliage for weddings with an informal feel.

For Students:
Family: Garryaceae.
Genus & Species: *Garrya elliptica*.
Native to: Western America.
Trivia: Named after Nicholas Garry, secretary to the Canadian based Hudson's Bay Company who took part in explorations of the Pacific North-west in the 1820's.

Gaultheria

Common Name: **Salal tips**

Availability: All year round.

Vase Life: 14–21 days.

Foliage Notes: An evergreen with thick, tough leaves, Gaultheria is common in coniferous forests where it forms dense thickets of foliage. Medium stem length.

Colour Range: Mid to bright green.

Conditioning:

- Ideal temperature range: 2–5°C (36–41°F).
- Re-cut stems, preferably with secateurs.
- Stand in clean water, flower food is not necessary.
- Change water every 4–5 days.
- Store away from direct heat and draughts.

General Information:

- Hardy, tough leaves with slightly toothed edges and a woody stem.
- Long-lasting foliage suitable for using in both vase designs and floral foam.
- **Texture:** Smooth.
- **Leaf Shape:** Oval.
- **Would complement:** A wide range of flowers with the exception of tropical blooms.

 Gaultheria shallon

In Design and Wedding Work:

Although this foliage will never win prizes for stylish looks, it is a good all-rounder, great for filling out hand-tied designs and for covering floral foam. Not delicate or attractive enough for more sophisticated bridal work, salal's fan shaped branches are handy and inexpensive for large arrangements and more rustic style vase and table designs. Its excellent vase life means that it is great value for money. Can be used in wired work.

For Students:

Family: Ericaceae.

Genus & Species: *Gaultheria shallon*.

Native to: North America.

Trivia: Gaultheria was introduced into Britain in 1828 where it became popular as ground cover for pheasants on large Victorian shooting estates.

Gossypium

Common Name: **Cotton, Upland cotton, Mexican cotton**

Availability: July–January with limited availability for the rest of the year.

Vase Life: 14–21 days. Can be dried.

Foliage Notes: Pronounced 'gos-SIP-ee-um'. A woody plant with alternate clumps of soft, fluffy cotton. Cultivated mainly for its seed fibre, which provides the raw material for the textile industry. Medium stem length.

Colour Range: Cotton wool white.

Conditioning:

- Ideal temperature range: 12–15°C (54–59°F).
- Re-cut stems, preferably with secateurs.
- Stand in clean, shallow water, flower food is not necessary.
- Change water every 4–5 days.
- Store away from direct heat and draughts.

General Information:

- Gossypium will dry very easily if left out of water.
- Long-lasting and suitable for using in both vase designs and floral foam.
- **Texture:** Fluffy.
- **Would complement:** Textured flowers and foliages, dried arrangements.

In Design and Wedding Work:
Not commonly seen in design work, Gossypium comes into its own at winter and Christmas time. The fluffy cotton 'buds' add great texture to wintry arrangements and give a subtle warmth to Christmas designs. It can be sprayed with gold or silver paint, although this should be done with care so as to not soak the cotton. As it dries, the stem will become more brittle. Use for decoration in churches and venues for Christmas weddings.

 Gossypium hirsutum

For Students:
Family: Malvaceae.
Genus & Species: *Gossypium hirsutum.*
Native to: Central America.
Trivia: There is evidence of cotton being cultivated in Mexico over 5,000 years ago. The source of its name is the word 'goz' which comes from Arabic and refers to a soft substance.

Grevillea

Common Name: **Grevillea**

Availability: September–March.

Vase Life: 14–21 days.

Foliage Notes: A large group of evergreen shrubs and trees, popular in gardens in the southern hemisphere. It can be grown in hothouses in colder climates. Medium stem length.

Colour Range: Mid-green with a contrasting underside.

Conditioning:

- Ideal temperature range: 2–5°C (36–41°F).
- Re-cut stems, preferably with secateurs.
- Stand in clean water, flower food is not necessary.
- Change water every 4–5 days.
- Store away from direct heat and draughts.

General Information:

- Often dyed in different colours, usually very bright and vibrant.
- Never leave Grevillea out of water as it dries out quickly.
- **Texture:** Spiky.
- **Leaf Shape:** Linear with a serrated edge.
- **Would complement:** Bright seasonal flowers such as Helianthus, Kniphofia and Celosia.

In Design and Wedding Work:

If using dyed Grevillea wear gloves if possible as the dye does come off quite easily, for this reason, avoid using in designs where it may be in contact with clothes. Too skinny to be a filler flower, its slim shape is more suited to setting off bolder flowers. Great for Halloween and bonfire night designs and arrangements for autumn and winter weddings. It can be rolled and wired into corsages, although it is a little fiddly.

 *Grevillea longifolia*

For Students:

Family: Proteaceae.

Genus & Species: *Grevillea longifolia.*

Native to: Australia.

Trivia: Grevillea flowers were a traditional favourite among Aborigines who enjoyed sampling the sweet tasting nectar.

Hebe

Common Name: **Hebe**

Availability: All year round.

Vase Life: 14–21 days.

Foliage Notes: A dense, evergreen shrub with small, regularly shaped leaves. Spikes of delicate flowers appear in the summer and autumn. Medium stem length.

Colour Range: Sage to bright green.

Conditioning:

- Ideal temperature range: 2–5°C (36–41°F).
- Re-cut stems, preferably with secateurs.
- Stand in clean, shallow water, flower food is not necessary.
- Change water every 4–5 days.
- Store away from direct heat and draughts.

General Information:

- Long-lasting, woody stemmed foliage suitable for using in vase designs and floral foam.
- **Texture:** Bushy.
- **Leaf Shape:** Elliptic/Oval.
- **Would complement:** Small, spring flowers such as Narcissus, Hellebore and Anemones.

Hebe rakaiensis

In Design and Wedding Work:

Hebe is a bushy, yet neat foliage, that fits in perfectly with the 'just picked from the garden' look. Use Hebe in traditional arrangements and small natural hand-tieds, it's not impressive enough to use as focal foliage but is very useful to fill out designs and hide holes! Hebe will complement delicate pastel shades such as lemons, pale blues and pinks, and is rather lovely when combined with spring flowers. Can be wired for corsages and buttonholes.

For Students:

Family: Plantaginaceae.

Genus & Species: *Hebe* sp.

Native to: Majority to New Zealand.

Trivia: It is thought that Hebe first arrived in New Zealand over 5 million years ago. It can be found in every environment on the islands.

Hedera

Availability: All year round, peaks September–April.

Vase Life: 14–21 days.

Foliage Notes: A familiar evergreen climber which can quickly become invasive if left unchecked. Robust and reliable, it has attractive berries in autumn. Long stem length.

Colour Range: Dark/light green also variegated cream, silver and yellow.

Conditioning:

- Ideal temperature range: 2–5°C (36–41°F).
- Re-cut stems, either with scissors or a sharp knife.
- Stand in clean, shallow water, flower food is not necessary.
- Change water every 4–5 days, store away from direct heat and draughts.

General Information:

- Long-lasting foliage suitable for using in vase designs, hand-tieds and floral foam.
- Ivy 'harvested' from roadsides will need washing and picking over before use.
- **Texture:** Smooth.
- **Leaf Shape:** Lobed/Ovate.
- **Would complement:** Autumn and winter flowers.

x2 *Hedera helix*

Hedera colchica 'Sulphur Heart'

In Design and Wedding Work:

Ivy has a multitude of uses; wind long lengths around hand-tieds and trail it from and around pedestal designs to increase their visual size for very little extra cost. Individual leaves can be wired to edge buttonholes and corsages. Ivy comes into its own in winter and Christmas designs where it is invaluable in table garlanding and door wreaths. Its berries add a lovely contrast to natural hand-tieds and arrangements.

Foliage Meaning: Fidelity, marriage.

For Students:

Family: Araliaceae.

Genus & Species: *Hedera* sp.

Native to: Europe & Western Asia.

Trivia: Ivy flowers are an important source of nectar for bees and insects in autumn. The berries which follow are enjoyed by birds, although they are poisonous to humans.

71

Hibiscus

Common Name: **Roselle, Jamaican red sorrel, Java jute**

Availability: September–December.

Vase Life: 7–10 days.

Foliage Notes: The attractive, fleshy fruit of the Hibiscus flower contain a number of seeds which are released when it reaches maturity. Medium stem length.

Colour Range: Red to pale pink with off-white markings.

Conditioning:

- Ideal temperature range: 2–5°C (36–41°F).
- Re-cut stems, preferably with secateurs.
- Stand in clean, shallow water, flower food is not necessary.
- Change water every 4–5 days.
- Store away from direct heat and draughts.

General Information:

- Handle carefully as the heads can be easily knocked off.
- Becomes slightly sticky to the touch as it matures.
- **Texture:** Rough.
- **Would complement:** Autumn flowers and fruits; Carthamus, Curcubita, Chrysanthemum.

In Design and Wedding Work:

With its erect stems and striking appearance, Hibiscus needs to be shown off in arrangements, not tucked away at the back. It will have more impact in modern and structured designs, although in the right colour scheme it would not look entirely out of place in large showy, traditional arrangements. Most suited to autumn and winter weddings, it is a little too stiff for informal bridal work, but would be perfect in vase designs. Unsuitable for wiring.

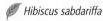 *Hibiscus sabdariffa*

For Students:

Family: Malvaceae.

Genus & Species: *Hibiscus sabdariffa.*

Native to: Tropical regions.

Trivia: In some tropical areas the slightly acidic fruits are used as a base for sauces and for making jellies, preserves and chutneys.

Hosta

Availability: April–October, peaks May–August.

Vase Life: 5–7 days.

Foliage Notes: Clump forming herbaceous plant, extremely popular in gardens due to its large decorative leaves and bell-like flowers that appear in early summer. Short stem length.

Colour Range: Mid to light green with cream/yellow margins.

Conditioning:

- Ideal temperature range: 2–5°C (36–41°F).
- Re-cut stems with a sharp knife or scissors.
- Stand in clean, shallow water, flower food is not necessary.
- Change water every 2–3 days.
- Store away from direct heat and draughts.

General Information:

- Hosta leaves are quite soft, take care when handling.
- More suitable for vase designs and hand-tieds as it can be awkward to anchor in floral foam.
- **Texture:** Ribbed.
- **Leaf Shape:** Ovate.
- **Would complement:** Classic flowers; rose, peony, Astilbe, lily-of-the-valley.

 Hosta 'Golden Tiara'

In Design and Wedding Work:

Hosta is an attractive foliage which can be used to form a natural collar around hand-tied designs and will enhance a focal area to great effect. Lovely for informal summer weddings they can also be wired and rolled with care. If using in floral foam cut the stem cleanly with a horizontal edge to help insert the end into the foam. Although this shrub is common in gardens, avoid using new, young leaves as they can wilt quickly after being cut.

For Students:

Family: Asparagaceae.

Genus & Species: *Hosta* sp.

Native to: Far East.

Trivia: Named in honour of the Austrian botanist Nicholas Thomas Host who was the first director of the botanical garden at the Belvedere Palace in Vienna.

73

Hydrangea

Common Name: **Hydrangea**

Availability: April–November, peaks May–October.

Vase Life: 7–14 days.

Foliage Notes: Attractive, sturdy leaves which have a design life of their own outside of providing a backdrop to the showy, mop headed blooms of this popular garden shrub. Medium stem length.

Colour Range: Bright green.

Conditioning:

- Ideal temperature range: 2–5°C (36–41°F).
- Re-cut stems, preferably with secateurs.
- Stand in clean, deep water with flower food.
- Change water every 4–5 days.
- Store away from direct heat and draughts.

General Information:

- Do not leave out of water for long periods.
- Long-lasting foliage suitable for using in both vase designs and floral foam.
- Texture: Bushy.
- Leaf Shape: Ovate.
- Would complement: Classic garden flowers; Aster, Sweet William, lupin and peony.

 *Hydrangea macrophylla*

In Design and Wedding Work:
Hydrangea foliage is often overlooked, which is a great shame as not only is it reliable and robust but it is good value for money as well. Use stems of Hydrangea to lengthen arrangements in floral foam and to fill out pedestal designs. It is a pleasing alternative to more commercial foliage, and cut into smaller pieces can be added into bridal posies and even wired into corsages with care. Always keep containers topped up with water.

For Students:
Family: Hydrangeaceae.
Genus & Species: *Hydrangea* sp.
Native to: Japan.
Trivia: First introduced into Europe in 1789 from the Far East, *H. macrophylla* is famous for being able to change colour from pink to blue depending on the pH value of the soil.

Ilex

Availability: October–December.

Vase Life: 10–15 days.

Foliage Notes: Quintessential Christmas foliage, the shiny, glossy leaves of holly are unmistakable. Clusters of bright berries complete the seasonal look. Medium stem length.

Colour Range: Dark green and variegated with pillar-box red berries.

 *Ilex aquifolium*

Conditioning:

- Ideal temperature range: 2–5°C (36–41°F).
- Re-cut stems, preferably with secateurs, handling with care.
- Stand in clean water, flower food is not necessary.
- Change water every 4–5 days, store away from direct heat and draughts.
- Remove all foliage in contact with water.

General Information:

- Avoid ingesting the berries, as they are mildly toxic.
- Woody stemmed, long-lasting foliage suitable for using in both vase designs and floral foam.
- **Texture:** Spiny/Glossy.
- **Leaf Shape:** Oval.
- **Would complement:** Seasonal winter foliage; mistletoe, spruce and pine.

Ilex aquifolium
'Silver Queen'

In Design and Wedding Work:
No Christmas design would be complete without a sprig of holly. Wonderful for door wreaths, fireplace garlands and table arrangements, its glossy foliage will enhance the rich reds and gold of Christmas colour themes. To guarantee berries, add in stems of *Ilex verticillata*. Not recommended in wired bridal work for obvious reasons, but can be added into bouquets if the stems are stripped with care. **Foliage Meaning:** Foresight.

For Students:
Family: Aquifoliaceae.

Genus & Species: *Ilex* sp.

Native to: S. Europe, N. Africa, S/W Asia.

Trivia: Holly is one of Britain's few native evergreen trees. In Pagan times it was placed in the home in winter as a hospitable gesture; it was also believed to repel evil spirits.

75

Jasminum

Common Name: **Jasmine**

Availability: September–December.

Vase Life: 7–14 days.

Foliage Notes: A vigorous climbing shrub with leaves that have a deceptively delicate appearance. Grown primarily for its fragrant flowers which are most pungent after dark. Long stem length.

Colour Range: Forest green.

Conditioning:

- Ideal temperature range: 2–5°C (36–41°F).
- Re-cut stems, handling with care, it's better to cut than pull the tendrils apart.
- Stand in clean water with flower food.
- Change water every 4–5 days.
- Store away from direct heat and draughts.

General Information:

- Jasmine appreciates a humid atmosphere, mist occasionally.
- Long-lasting foliage suitable for using in both vase designs and floral foam.
- **Texture:** Feathery.
- **Leaf Shape:** Pinnate.
- **Would complement:** Pretty, delicate flowers; spray roses, Freesia, Phlox or Veronica.

 *Jasminum nudiflorum*

In Design and Wedding Work:
Jasmine is absolutely gorgeous for a late summer, early autumn wedding. The pretty, delicate leaves can be wound around the edges of hand-ties to add style and subtle movement or used to cascade from shower bouquets. Trail jasmine from pedestals and long 'n' low designs to soften edges and create volume. More robust than it looks, jasmine can be added into corsages, boutonnières and more ornate wired work. **Foliage Meaning:** Amiability.

For Students:
Family: Oleaceae.
Genus & Species: *Jasminum* sp.
Native to: Himalayas/W. China.
Trivia: Jasmine is an important part of many rituals in India, including marriage ceremonies and festivals. It is widely used in the home for regular worship.

Kochia

Availability: September–February.

Vase Life: 7–10 days.

Foliage Notes: Pronounced 'Ko-sha'. A hardy, drought tolerant annual capable of growing up to 2m (6'). Common in the United States where it is grown as forage for cattle. Short stem length.

Colour Range: Silvery grey-green.

Conditioning:

- Ideal temperature range: 2–5°C (36–41°F).
- Re-cut stems, preferably with secateurs, handling with care.
- Stand in clean water with flower food, ensuring leaves don't touch the water.
- Change water every 2–3 days, don't overcrowd containers.
- Store away from direct heat and draughts.

General Information:

- To ensure maximum vase life give Kochia plenty of room and air circulation.
- Prone to foliage drop and can get a little slimy if not conditioned properly.
- **Texture:** Woolly.
- **Leaf Shape:** Oval.
- **Would complement:** Pink and purple early spring flowers; Anemone, Narcissus, Freesia.

In Design and Wedding Work:

Kochia has a lovely soft appearance and is particularly suitable for spring flowers where it will add line and texture to natural hand-tieds and arrangements. Choose a pastel scheme to make the most of its delicate colouring, although it works just as well with fresh limes, whites and deep yellows. Kochia will last well in arrangements in floral foam, but make sure that the foliage doesn't touch wet surfaces. Can be wired with care.

Kochia scoparia
(Syn. *Bassia scoparia*)

For Students:

Family: Chenopodiaceae/ Amaranthaceae.

Genus & Species: *Kochia scoparia*.

Native to: Asia.

Trivia: In the genus Kochia since 1809, the botanist A. J. Scott reclassified the plant in 1978 into Bassia, a genus of the Amaranthus family.

77

Laurus

Common Name: **Bay, Sweet bay, Poet's laurel**

Availability: All year round.

Vase Life: 10–21 days.

Foliage Notes: A bushy evergreen tree with leathery, aromatic leaves that have a variety of culinary uses. Small yellow flowers are followed by glossy black berries in the autumn. Medium stem length.

Colour Range: Dark green.

Conditioning:

- Ideal temperature range: 2–5°C (36–41°F).
- Re-cut stems, preferably with secateurs or a sharp knife.
- Stand in clean, fresh water, flower food is not necessary.
- Change water every 4–5 days.
- Store away from direct heat and draughts.

General Information:

- Hardy, tough leaves with slightly toothed edges and a woody stem.
- Long-lasting foliage suitable for using in both vase designs and floral foam.
- **Texture:** Smooth.
- **Leaf Shape:** Ovate.
- **Would complement:** Cottage garden flowers; herbs, roses, Sweet William or Hellebores.

Laurus nobilis

In Design and Wedding Work:

Use bay as the main or focal foliage in designs where its delicate, aromatic leaves can be appreciated. Lovely for textured work and when fresh its leaves are robust enough to be layered and pinned as a base material. At Christmas time add it into wreaths, garlanding and swags. Clipped bay trees are also popular as free standing decorations at weddings. Bay can be a little sticky when cut, so use in wired work with care.

Foliage meaning: Glory.

For Students:

Family: Lauraceae.

Genus & Species: *Laurus nobilis*.

Native to: Mediterranean.

Trivia: The Chinese name for laurel translates literally to "moon-laurel" as, according to Chinese folklore, there is a great laurel tree which grows on the moon.

Leucadendron

Common Name: **Leucadendron, Conebush**

Availability: March to August with limited availability at other times.

Vase Life: 14–21 days.

Foliage Notes: Pronounced 'Lou-KA-den-dron.' A bushy shrub with hard, scale-like leaves. Grown for its ornamental foliage, its flower is relatively insignificant. Medium stem length.

Colour Range: Lime green to deep burgundy.

Conditioning:

- Ideal temperature range: 5–8°C (41–46°F).
- Re-cut stems, preferably with secateurs or a sharp knife.
- Stand in clean, fresh water with flower food.
- Change water every 4–5 days and store away from direct heat and draughts.

General Information:

- Do not store for long periods in the dark.
- Long-lasting foliage suitable for using in both vase designs and floral foam.
- **Texture:** Bushy.
- **Leaf Shape:** Lance.
- **Would complement:** Tropical/bright flowers; Anthurium, Heliconia, Helianthus.

Leucadendron platyspermum

In Design and Wedding Work:

A popular foliage for hand-tieds and arrangements, Leucadendron is seen at its best when used in more limited, contemporary work, for this reason it is useful for contract and corporate designs. Its tall sturdy stems add height and line to large arrangements and its range of colours make it suitable for practically any scheme. Create areas of interest by grouping together heads of Leucadendron in textured designs. Its scaly leaves can be glued (although it's fiddly) as an alternative to basing.

For Students:

Family: Proteaceae.

Genus & Species: *Leucadendron* sp.

Native to: South Africa.

Trivia: The name Leucadendron comes from the Greek words 'leukos' for white and 'dendron' for tree, referring to the silvery-coloured foliage of some varieties.

79

Leucobryum

Common Name: **Bun moss, Pin cushion moss**

Availability: All year round.

Vase Life: 21 days plus.

Foliage Notes: Pronounced 'leu-CO-bri-um'. A soft, mounded moss which grows on a variety of surfaces from rich, acidic soils to barren, sandy locations.

Colour Range: Mid to pale green.

Conditioning:

- Ideal temperature range: 2–5°C (36–41°F).
- Usually delivered in a polystyrene box which should ideally be stored in a cool room.
- Mist occasionally and cover with plastic to keep it fresh.
- Store away from direct heat and draughts.

General Information:

- The depth of colour of bun moss depends on its moisture content.
- Keep moss moist to avoid it breaking up.
- **Texture:** Rough.
- **Would complement:** Spring flowers, planted designs.

In Design and Wedding Work:

Bun moss is indispensable for textured designs and tributes. Pin into soil or floral foam with wire 'hairpins', use coated wires where possible to avoid rusting. It can be glued but needs to be completely dry first, bear in mind it becomes more fragile when dry. Handy for covering soil and retaining moisture in planted designs, it is also an interesting alternative for a basing material. Large quantities of bun moss can be grouped together to create 'pathways' through floral installations.

Leucobryum glaucum

For Students:

Family: Leucobryaceae.

Genus & Species: *Leucobryum glaucum.*

Native to: N. temperate areas.

Trivia: Bryology is the branch of botany concerned with the study of mosses, liverworts and hornworts. According to bryologists, there are 122 species of Leucobryum worldwide.

Leucothoe

Availability: August–April.

Vase Life: 7–14 days.

Foliage Notes: Pronounced 'Loo-CO-tho'. Hardy, ornamental garden shrub which provides excellent ground cover. Its distinctively coloured leaves make it very popular with gardeners. Medium stem length.

Colour Range: Forest green, lime/crimson in autumn.

Conditioning:

- Ideal temperature range: 2–5°C (36–41°F).
- Re-cut stems with secateurs or a sharp knife.
- Stand in clean water, flower food is not necessary.
- Change water every 4–5 days.
- Store away from direct heat and draughts.

General Information:

- Hardy, shiny leaves with a woody stem.
- Long-lasting foliage suitable for using in both vase designs and floral foam.
- **Texture:** Bushy.
- **Leaf Shape:** Lance.
- **Would complement:** Garden flowers such as Aster, Salvia and Sweet William.

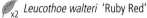 *Leucothoe walteri* 'Ruby Red'

In Design and Wedding Work:

Gorgeous foliage whose graceful, arching stems lend themselves to country style garden arrangements. Leucothoe is a showy foliage and a little pricey for a simple filler, instead use it to enhance focal areas. For weddings, add into garlanding and swags to strengthen a particular colour scheme. Leaves are too soft for wiring, but Leucothoe would be lovely in natural tied posies, especially for an autumn wedding.

For Students:

Family: Ericaceae.

Genus & Species: *Leucothoe* sp.

Native to: Mediterranean/W. Europe.

Trivia: Cold winters intensify Leucothoe, enhancing the copper colour of its foliage. It keeps this colour over the winter into the spring.

81

Ligularia

Common Name: **Leopard plant, Elephant ears**

Availability: June–October.

Vase Life: 7–10 days.

Foliage Notes: A large and impressive perennial which prefers a boggy spot in the garden. It has tall spikes of yellow/orange flowers in summer. Medium stem length.

Colour Range: Moss green.

Conditioning:

- Ideal temperature range: 2–5°C (36–41°F).
- Re-cut stems with scissors or a sharp knife.
- Stand in clean water with flower food.
- Change water every 2–3 days.
- Store away from direct heat and draughts.

General Information:

- Suitable for using in both vase designs and floral foam, but handle stems with care.
- **Texture:** Smooth.
- **Leaf Shape:** Reniform.
- **Would complement:** Flowers with strong form such as Gerbera or Curcuma.

 Ligularia 'Gregynog Gold'

In Design and Wedding Work:
An unusual foliage, not something that you would normally expect to see in your average arrangement. Ligularia's large, lily pad like leaves lend themselves to more contemporary designs either in foam or as a hand-tied. Excellent focal foliage, if using in floral foam ensure that the container is kept topped up as they will wilt quickly if out of contact with water. Not suitable for wired bridal work.

For Students:
Family: Asteraceae.
Genus & Species: *Ligularia* sp.
Native to: Eastern/Central Asia.
Trivia: Ligularia's name comes from the Latin for 'strap' which refers to its distinctive flower spike.

Ligustrum

Availability: August–January.

Vase Life: 7–10 days.

Foliage Notes: Semi-evergreen shrub with small white panicles of flowers that are followed by shiny black berries in autumn. Britain's most common hedging plant. Medium stem length.

Colour Range: Dark green.

Conditioning:

- Ideal temperature range: 2–5°C (36–41°F).
- Re-cut stems, preferably with secateurs.
- Stand in clean water, flower food is not necessary.
- Change water every 4–5 days.
- Store away from direct heat and draughts.

General Information:

- Foliage is suitable for using in both vase designs and floral foam.
- **Texture:** Bushy.
- **Leaf Shape:** Oval.
- **Would complement:** Traditional flowers: Chrysanthemums, carnations and Alstroemeria.

In Design and Wedding Work:

It's difficult to see where privet would be welcome in a design. Certainly customers receiving it as part of a gift would probably feel more than a little short changed. Stiff and unwieldy, the most appropriate use for it would be foliage edging on a funeral tribute or for filling out large pedestal arrangements in traditional designs. It has a tendency to dry out so containers should be topped up and foliage sprayed on a regular basis.

Ligustrum ovalifolium

For Students:

Family: Oleaceae.

Genus & Species: *Ligustrum ovalifolium*.

Native to: Japan.

Trivia: Despite its commonplace appearance *Ligustrum ovalifolium* 'Aureum' has gained an RHS Award of Garden Merit.

Liriope

Common Name: **Lily turf, Lily grass**

Availability: All year round.

Vase Life: 12–20 days.

Foliage Notes: Pronounced 'Le-RI-oh-pee'. Evergreen herbaceous perennial which forms into large spreading clumps of attractive grasses with slim arching leaves. Medium stem length.

Colour Range: Bottle green.

Conditioning:

- Ideal temperature range: 2–5°C (36–41°F).
- Re-cut stems, preferably with scissors or a sharp knife.
- Stand in clean water with flower food.
- Change water every 4–5 days.
- Store away from direct heat and draughts.

General Information:

- Long-lasting foliage suitable for using in both vase designs and floral foam.
- **Texture:** Smooth.
- **Leaf Shape:** Strap.
- **Would complement:** Contemporary flowers; Allium, Gerbera or Agapanthus.

In Design and Wedding Work:

A sturdy grass which can be manipulated in a number of ways; rolled, knotted or woven and can be easily secured by glue or decorative pins. Left at full length, lily grass will add instant volume to arrangements and provide an elegant line seamlessly linking one element of a design with another. Use lily grass to add movement to hand-tied designs and make the most of its flexibility by incorporating it into corsages and buttonholes.

 x2 *Liriope gigantea*

For Students:

Family: Asparagaceae.

Genus & Species: *Liriope gigantea.*

Native to: Japan.

Trivia: In China, Liriope is known as "book tape herb" as it was once grown in gardens to use as book marks when paper was a rare commodity.

Liriope

Common Name: **China grass, Big blue lily turf**

Availability: All year round.

Vase Life: 10–18 days.

Foliage Notes: Pronounced 'Le-RI-oh-pee'. Evergreen perennial with small violet-purple flowers carried in dense, erect spikes which are followed by black berries in autumn. Medium stem length.

Colour Range: Light green with cream stripes.

Conditioning:

- Ideal temperature range: 2–5°C (36–41°F).
- Re-cut stems, preferably with scissors.
- Stand in clean water with flower food.
- Change water every 4–5 days.
- Store away from direct heat and draughts.

General Information:

- Long-lasting foliage suitable for using in both vase designs and floral foam.
- **Texture:** Smooth.
- **Leaf Shape:** Strap.
- **Would complement:** Delicate spring and summer flowers.

In Design and Wedding Work:

Although delicate in appearance, China grass is surprisingly robust. Most effective when used in groups rather than singly, it can, as lily grass, be woven and manipulated in numerous different ways and is excellent for modern hand-tieds and funeral tributes. China grass will also add movement and line to natural tied posies and bridal shower bouquets. Groups of grass wired into garlanding will make even the most mundane swag sparkle. Indispensable in wired work for adding designer touches to boutonnières and corsages.

Liriope muscari

For Students:

Family: Asparagaceae.

Genus & Species: *Liriope muscari*.

Native to: Far East.

Trivia: Liriope grows as an understory plant in China, Japan, and Korea where it can be found in shady forests at elevations of 1000–1500m (3200–5000').

Magnolia

Common Name: **Magnolia, Bull bay**

Availability: February–May.

Vase Life: 2–3 days.

Foliage Notes: A striking ornamental tree with showy star-shaped flowers that appear in spring, often ahead of its leaves. Flowers are sometimes fragrant. Tall stem length.

Colour Range: Rich green with a rust coloured underside.

Conditioning:

- Ideal temperature range: 2–5°C (36–41°F).
- Woody stemmed, re-cut with secateurs.
- Stand in clean, shallow water.
- Change water daily.
- Store away from direct heat and draughts.

General Information:

- Magnolia doesn't store well, use within 24 hours of cutting.
- The brown undersides of the leaves are a contrast to the green upper.
- **Texture:** Woody.
- **Leaf Shape:** Elliptic.
- **Would complement:** Striking, single flowers such as Agapanthus, Allium or lily.

x4 Magnolia grandiflora

In Design and Wedding Work:
Usually sold commercially as bare boughs, Magnolia can be expensive but if you can obtain it from the garden, then large lengths of this ornamental tree are very impressive. Keep floral foam topped up and re-cut stems regularly if using in vases. Individual leaves are strong enough to be wired and can be pinned and layered as a textured surface for modern bridal designs. Skeletonised and bleached leaves are also popular in design work.
Foliage Meaning: Love of Nature.

For Students:
Family: Magnoliaceae.
Genus & Species: *Magnolia grandiflora.*
Native to: S/E Asia and Americas.
Trivia: Magnolia was named for the French botanist, Pierre Magnol in 1703. Fossilised Magnolia has been found dating back 20 million years.

Mahonia

Common Name: **Oregon Grape**

Availability: All year round.

Vase Life: 5–7 days.

Foliage Notes: Evergreen shrub with spiny, leathery leaves popular in public planting schemes as it is tough, vigorous and spreads easily. Bears bright yellow flowers in late winter. Medium stem length.

Colour Range: Moss green maturing to burgundy.

Conditioning:

- Ideal temperature range: 2–5°C (36–41°F).
- Woody stemmed, re-cut with secateurs, handling with care.
- Stand in clean water, flower food is not necessary.
- Change water every 2–3 days.
- Store away from direct heat and draughts.

General Information:

- Doesn't store well, use as soon as possible after cutting.
- Can be used in both vase designs and floral foam.
- **Texture:** Leathery.
- **Leaf Shape:** Pinnate.
- **Would complement:** Chrysanthemum blooms, Dahlia or Hydrangea.

 Mahonia aquifolium

In Design and Wedding Work:

Although extremely useful for inexpensively bulking out large arrangements, Mahonia does have the disadvantage of being extremely spiky. Consequently it is not foliage which is used a great deal commercially, but if you are prepared to either wear gardening gloves or patiently trim off the sharp tips of the leaves Mahonia is reliable and interesting texturally. Not suitable in hand-tied bouquets or bridal work for obvious reasons!

For Students:

Family: Berberidaceae.

Genus & Species: *Mahonia* sp.

Native to: Western North America.

Trivia: The juice from the purplish black berries can be fermented to make wine.

Malus

Common Name: **Crab apple**

Availability: August–December, peaks September–December.

Vase Life: 5–7 days.

Foliage Notes: Compact deciduous tree that has showy flowers in spring followed by distinctive clusters of glossy fruits that persist well into the winter. Tall stem length.

Colour Range: Red/orange.

Conditioning:

- Ideal temperature range: 2–5°C (36–41°F).
- Woody stemmed, re-cut with secateurs.
- Stand in clean water, flower food is not necessary.
- Change water every 2–3 days.
- Store away from direct heat and draughts.

General Information:

- Malus can either be bought as fruiting branches, or as loose fruits in containers.
- Handle carefully as the fruits are easy to dislodge.
- Removing the leaves will improve the appearance of stems.
- **Texture:** Smooth/Shiny.
- **Would complement:** Richly coloured autumn flowers.

Malus x robusta 'Red Sentinel'

In Design and Wedding Work:

Marvellous for autumn arrangements, Malus is very effective in large designs, where its vibrant colours can be appreciated. If using in floral foam, ensure containers are kept topped up and the stems are firmly anchored. If adding into vases it can be a little unwieldy without the security of foam to hold it in place. Remove any fruits or foliage below water level and keep for scattering on tables. Crab apples can be threaded on wires and pinned into arrangements with care.

For Students:

Family: Rosaceae.

Genus & Species: *Malus* sp.

Native to: N. hemisphere.

Trivia: Crab apples are often used as pollinators in apple orchards. To encourage bees, branches are put into buckets and placed near to hives.

Miscanthus

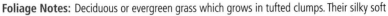

Availability: August–October.

Vase Life: 7–14 days.

Foliage Notes: Deciduous or evergreen grass which grows in tufted clumps. Their silky soft foliage changes colour as the seasons mature. Medium stem length.

Colour Range: Dusky pink to chocolate brown.

Conditioning:

- Ideal temperature range: 2–5°C (36–41°F).
- Re-cut stems with scissors, handling with care.
- Stand in clean water with flower food.
- Change water every 4–5 days.
- Store away from direct heat and draughts.

General Information:

- Long-lasting, suitable for using in both vase designs and floral foam.
- **Texture:** Feathery.
- **Shape:** Linear.
- **Would complement:** Summer or autumn flowers rich colours and textures.

In Design and Wedding Work:

This attractive ornamental grass will give wonderful movement, line and texture to designs. For maximum effect group in twos or threes. Handle gently because the stems can bend easily. Miscanthus' delicate form can get overpowered in larger arrangements; it is most effective in smaller, more intimate designs. Use in natural bridal tieds for summer weddings which would be perfect for this lovely grass.

x3 *Miscanthus sinensis*

For Students:

Family: Poaceae.

Genus & Species: *Miscanthus sinensis*.

Native to: Africa & S. Asia.

Trivia: Very popular as an ornamental grass in Japan, where its fibrous qualities also make it an excellent material for making paper.

Monstera

Common Name: Swiss cheese plant, Mexican breadfruit plant

Availability: All year round.

Vase Life: 12–21 days.

Foliage Notes: A creeping vine found in tropical rain forests. Rooting themselves in tree trunks, they are capable of growing up to 20m (60'). Short stem length.

Colour Range: Dark glossy green.

Conditioning:

- Ideal temperature range: 12–15°C (54–59°F).
- Re-cut stems at an angle with a sharp knife.
- Stand in clean, shallow water with flower food.
- Change water every 4–5 days.
- Store away from direct heat and draughts.

General Information:

- Hardy, tough leaves with deeply cut margins.
- Long-lasting foliage suitable for using in both vase designs and floral foam.
- **Texture:** Leathery.
- **Leaf Shape:** Heart with deep cut margins.
- **Would complement:** Tropical flowers; Strelitzia, Heliconia or Protea.

x3 *Monstera deliciosa*

In Design and Wedding Work:

Bold and flamboyant, Monstera is not a leaf to fade modestly into the background! Fantastic for large, showy arrangements, use it to emphasis focal areas and add a touch of drama. In modern structural works give it its own space as an integral part of the design. Smaller Monstera leaves make excellent collars for hand-tied bouquets. Not a leaf commonly associated with wedding work, although for brides with a tropical theme it would be ideal.

For Students:

Family: Araceae.

Genus & Species: *Monstera deliciosa*.

Native to: Mexico & Central America.

Trivia: Monstera have edible fruits, hence 'deliciosa'. In Peru the robust aerial roots of the plant were once used to make baskets.

Myrica

Availability: November–April.

Vase Life: 15–30 days.

Foliage Notes: A deciduous shrub which can grow up to two metres tall. Attractive catkins in winter are followed by fleshy fruit which has a number of medicinal and food uses. Short stem length.

Colour Range: Reddish brown.

Conditioning:

- Ideal temperature range: 2–5°C (36–41°F).
- Myrica doesn't need to stand in water, keep in dry storage until needed.
- Store away from direct heat and draughts.

General Information:

- Extremely long-lasting suitable for using in both vase designs and floral foam.
- Myrica can be used more than once, simply swill off stems and dry off thoroughly.
- **Texture:** Rough.
- **Would complement:** Small stemmed flowers in Christmas and spring designs.

In Design and Wedding Work:

Delicate with a twig-like appearance Myrica has great texture and is particularly effective in spring designs where it would coordinate well with both pastel and more vibrant colour schemes. Whether included in a simple hand-tied or a more complicated structured design Myrica will add an attractive slender line. Great for Christmas, wire Myrica into bundles for more impact before adding into swags and wreaths. Small pieces can used in wired work.

 Myrica gale

For Students:

Family: Myricaceae.

Genus & Species: *Myrica gale*.

Native to: N/W Europe & N. America.

Trivia: Myrica has a huge number of different applications from acne treatment to insect repellent. A brewing company in Canada make 'Bog Water', strong ale made with Myrica.

91

Myrtus

Common Name: **Myrtle**

Availability: February–April, October–November.

Vase Life: 10–15 days.

Foliage Notes: An erect, evergreen, aromatic shrub with attractive cup-shaped flowers and edible blue-black berries. Medium stem length.

Colour Range: Dark green.

Conditioning:

- Ideal temperature range: 2–5°C (36–41°F).
- Re-cut stems, preferably with secateurs or a sharp knife.
- Stand in clean water with flower food.
- Change water every 4–5 days.
- Store away from direct heat and draughts.

General Information:

- Hardy, tough leaves with a woody stem.
- Long-lasting foliage suitable for using in both vase designs and floral foam.
- **Texture:** Spiky.
- **Leaf Shape:** Ovate.
- **Would complement:** Traditional flowers such as carnations, lisianthus or roses.

Myrtus communis

In Design and Wedding Work:

A traditional foliage, associated with royal weddings ever since Queen Victoria added a sprig into her bouquet in 1840. Myrtle would still be a lovely addition to bridal work, in both natural tieds and more formal bouquets. Its aromatic foliage makes it attractive for brides looking for scent as well as colour and it would complement autumn bouquets in particular. Great for foliage edging tributes, backing tied sheaves and for giving line and structure to more traditional designs.

For Students:

Family: Myrtaceae.

Genus & Species: *Myrtus communis.*

Native to: Mediterranean regions.

Trivia: Saharan myrtle (*M. nivellei*) grows almost exclusively in sparse woodland in the centre of the Sahara Desert. It is listed as an endangered species.

Nelumbo

Availability: All year round.

Vase Life: 5–7 days.

Foliage Notes: An aquatic plant with large showy flowers that bear a close resemblance to water lilies. It grows in pond margins and shallow water and can spread up to 1.5m (5'). Medium stem length.

Colour Range: Bright green.

Conditioning:

- Ideal temperature range: 12–15°C (54–59°F).
- Re-cut stems with care.
- Stand in clean water with flower food.
- Change water every 2–3 days.
- Store away from direct heat and draughts as this can turn the heads black.

General Information:

- The heads damage easily so handle with care.
- Suitable for using in both vase designs and floral foam.
- Heads can be dried and sprayed with paint.
- **Texture:** Pitted.
- **Would complement:** Interesting, exotic flowers; Curcuma, Cymbidium or Anthurium.

In Design and Wedding Work:

A fascinating plant which never fails to go unnoticed. Its unique shaped head is perfect for adding a touch of pizazz to contemporary work, use full length in structured hand-tieds or wire individual heads into textured tributes. For adventurous brides who are looking for something a little different it can be added into natural bridal tieds and contemporary shower bouquets. Consider dried heads sprayed gold and silver for Christmas arrangements.

 *Nelumbo nucifera*

For Students:

Family: Nelumbonaceae.

Genus & Species: *Nelumbo nucifera.*

Native to: Asia & N. Australia.

Trivia: An iconic plant, which has been revered as a divine symbol for over 5,000 years. Lotus is the National Flower of Egypt, India and Vietnam.

93

Nephrolepis

Common Name: **Sword fern**

Availability: All year round, peaks December–September.

Vase Life: 7–14 days.

Foliage Notes: Pronounced 'Nef-ro-LEP-is'. A popular evergreen houseplant with attractive arching fronds. If grown outside it requires warm temperatures and protection from frost. Medium stem length.

Colour Range: Light green.

Conditioning:

- Ideal temperature range: 12–15°C (54–59°F).
- Re-cut stems, preferably with scissors.
- Stand in clean, fresh water with flower food.
- Change water every 4–5 days.
- Store away from direct heat and draughts.

General Information:

- Brown edges on fronds can be carefully trimmed off with scissors.
- Suitable for using in both vase designs and floral foam.
- **Texture:** Rippled.
- **Leaf Shape:** Pinnate.
- **Would complement:** Both traditional and tropical flowers.

 *Nephrolepis exaltata*

In Design and Wedding Work:

The pretty delicate fronds of sword fern are incredibly versatile, equally at home in traditional or modern designs. It will add elegant length and line to tributes and arrangements; group it in twos or threes for more impact. Use it to edge natural hand-tied posies to give subtle movement. Sword fern can also be looped and manipulated with care. It can also be incorporated into wired work, but needs gentle handling as stems can snap easily. **Foliage Meaning:** Fascination.

For Students:

Family: Nephrolepidaceae.

Genus & Species: *Nephrolepis exaltata*.

Native to: Tropical regions.

Trivia: Found growing naturally in humid swamps and forests, the delicate fronds of Nephrolepis are capable of reaching up to 1m (3') in length.

Nigella

Availability: June–December, peaks June–October.

Vase Life: 5–7 days.

Foliage Notes: The dried fruit heads of *N. damascena* are attractive in their own right, with their papery appearance and delicate, feathery leaves. Medium stem length.

Colour Range: Parchment with pale crimson markings.

Conditioning:

- Ideal temperature range: 2–5°C (36–41°F).
- Re-cut stems with scissors, handling with care.
- Stand in clean, shallow water, flower food is not necessary.
- Change water every 2–3 days.
- Store away from direct heat and draughts.

General Information:

- Nigella is a water polluter; remove any foliage in contact with water.
- Not ideal for storing as stems will rot quickly if left standing in water for too long.
- Handle carefully as they are very fragile.
- **Texture:** Feathery.
- **Would complement:** Delicate summer flowers such as oregano, scabious and Phlox.

In Design and Wedding Work:

Popular in dried designs, Nigella heads can also be added into fresh arrangements successfully. Gorgeous for late summer, early autumn weddings, where they will complement berries, herbs and similarly seasonal materials, use grouped for maximum impact. Not really suitable for arrangements in floral foam as the stems are weak, but can be added into hand-tied bouquets. If drying Nigella, hang them upside down to keep the stems straight.

Flower Meaning: Perplexity.

Nigella damascena

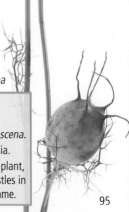

For Students:

Family: Ranunculaceae.

Genus & Species: *Nigella damascena*.

Native to: Mediterranean/SW Asia.

Trivia: A popular cottage garden plant, the lacy bracts that the flower nestles in are responsible for its common name.

95

Ophiopogon

Common Name: **Lilyturf, Black mondo**

Availability: All year round.

Vase Life: 7–14 days.

Foliage Notes: Pronounced 'oh-FEE-oh-po-gon'. Evergreen perennial with small bell-shaped white or mauve flowers in summer, followed by glossy black berries in autumn. Short stem length.

Colour Range: Dark purple maturing to black.

Conditioning:

- Ideal temperature range: 2–5°C (36–41°F).
- Stand in clean shallow water with flower food.
- Change water every 4–5 days.
- Store away from direct heat and draughts.

General Information:

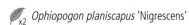 *Ophiopogon planiscapus* 'Nigrescens'

- If taking cuttings from a plant, condition for a couple of hours before use.
- **Texture:** Smooth.
- **Leaf Shape:** Strap.
- **Would complement:** Small, delicate flowers, try Hellebore, Muscari or Paphiopedilum.

In Design and Wedding Work:

An interesting and unusual black plant, not something commonly available as a commercial cut foliage but easy to obtain from garden centres. The leaves are quite short, so will need to be extended by wire if extra length is required in designs. Most suitable for modern, contemporary work, it can be added into bridal bouquets, boutonnières and corsages for an unusual colour contrast. It is a tough grass, so can be manipulated and/or woven successfully.

For Students:

Family: Asparagaceae.

Genus & Species: *Ophiopogon planiscapus.*

Native to: Asia.

Trivia: In Chinese Medicine *O. japonicus* is used to treat yin deficiency. It is supposed to nourish the yin of the stomach, heart and lungs and quiet irritability.

Panicum

Availability: April–November, peaks May–October.

Vase Life: 7–10 days.

Foliage Notes: Either annual or perennial, Panicum grass has narrow leaves and attractive, finely branched feathery spikelets in late summer/autumn. Medium stem length.

Colour Range: Fresh green.

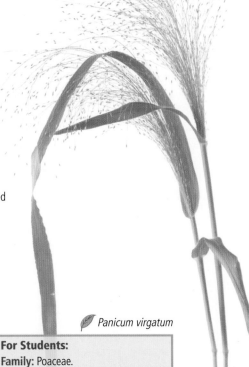

Conditioning:

- Ideal temperature range: 12–15°C (54–59°F).
- Re-cut stems with scissors, handling with care.
- Stand in clean water with flower food.
- Change water every 4–5 days.
- Store away from direct heat and draughts.

General Information:

- Leaves can become untidy as they age, trim off damaged areas with scissors.
- Suitable for using in both vase designs and floral foam.
- **Texture:** Feathery.
- **Leaf Shape:** Lance.
- **Would complement:** Natural, uncomplicated flowers; Helenium, Astrantia or cornflower.

Panicum virgatum

In Design and Wedding Work:
This delicate grass will add a lovely lightness and movement to hand-tied designs and natural tied posies. It can be used in floral foam but insert with care as stems can bend easily. Panicum looks great in summer and autumn bridal work, combine it with berries, rose hips and poppy heads for a seasonal harvest theme. If adding into large arrangements it is more effective grouped than used singly. Can be wired with care.

For Students:
Family: Poaceae.

Genus & Species: *Panicum virgatum*.

Native to: North America.

Trivia: A native of the prairies of the Midwestern states, it is sometimes used as a substitute for straw, and has been used for making straw bale houses.

97

Papaver

Common Name: **Poppy**

Availability: May–October, peaks June–October.

Vase Life: 7–10 days.

Foliage Notes: An iconic garden plant, the brightly coloured papery petals of the poppy are short lived, but its distinctive seed head gives it a second life. Medium stem length.

Colour Range: Sage green.

Conditioning:

- Ideal temperature range: 2–5°C (36–41°F).
- Re-cut stems handling with care as they are quite delicate.
- Stand in clean water, flower food is not necessary.
- Change water every 4–5 days.
- Store away from direct heat and draughts.

General Information:

- If harvesting pods from the garden, choose heads that are showing a hint of green.
- Beware of the milky sap from freshly harvested stems as it can be an irritant.
- Don't overcrowd vases as the heads damage easily.
- **Texture:** Smooth/Ribbed.
- **Would complement:** Cottage garden flowers; Nigella, Helianthus or Eryngium.

Papaver orientale

In Design and Wedding Work:

Poppy seed heads will add an extra dimension to autumn flower arrangements and tied designs, for impact use in pairs or groups rather than singly. Heads can be sprayed gold or silver and added into Christmas arrangements. Stems are hollow; a wire inserted inside the stem will keep them rigid. Try cutting the heads in half to display the intricate interior, or you can 'peel' poppy heads like an orange with care! If drying, remove all foliage and hang upside down in small groups in an area with good air circulation.

For Students:

Family: Papaveraceae.

Genus & Species: *Papaver* sp.

Native to: Central Asia.

Trivia: It was believed that when poppies grew in fields, they would bring forth a good crop – hence the term 'corn poppy.'

Common Name: Passion flower, Passion vine

Availability: All year round.

Vase Life: 7–14 days.

Foliage Notes: A tender climbing vine, usually evergreen with showy flowers and conspicuous fruits which are edible in some species. Medium stem length.

Colour Range: Dark glossy green.

Conditioning:

- Ideal temperature range: 2–5°C (36–41°F).
- Handle carefully as stems can easily tangle.
- Change water every 4–5 days.
- Store away from direct heat and draughts.

General Information:

- If using foliage from a plant cut, rather than pull, as this minimises damage.
- Suitable for using in both vase designs and floral foam.
- **Texture:** Bushy.
- **Leaf Shape:** Palmate.
- **Would complement:** Summer flowers; Peony, Hydrangea or stocks.

In Design and Wedding Work:

Passiflora is unusual and not generally found as a commercially cut foliage, but plants are easy to obtain from garden centres. It would make a lovely and dramatic addition to large designs, use it to trail elegantly from pedestals or wrap around the exterior of tall vases. It can also be used as a collar for hand-tied posies or woven through structural arrangements where it would complement bold and vibrant flowers.

Flower Meaning: Religious superstition.

Passiflora caerulea

For Students:

Family: Passifloraceae.

Genus & Species: *Passiflora caerulea.*

Native to: South America.

Trivia: The passionflower bee is a solitary insect that feeds solely from the nectar of the yellow passion flower *P. lutea*, found in the Eastern United States.

99

Pennisetum

Availability: March–November, peaks May–November.

Vase Life: 7–14 days.

Foliage Notes: Pronounced 'Pen-e-see-tum'. Clump forming, tufted grass with flowering panicles that gradually change colour from summer to autumn. Medium stem length.

Colour Range: Silver-grey to crimson-pink.

Conditioning:

- Ideal temperature range: 2–5°C (36–41°F).
- Re-cut stems with scissors, stand in clean water with flower food.
- Change water every 4–5 days.
- Store away from direct heat and draughts.

General Information:

- Heads are liable to bend, handle carefully.
- Don't overcrowd containers.
- **Texture:** Feathery.
- **Leaf Shape:** Linear.
- **Would complement:** Simple flowers; Leucanthemum, Liatris or Papaver.

In Design and Wedding Work:

A showy and unmistakable grass, Pennisetum is great for creating strong textural notes in hand-tieds and arrangements. Use carefully in floral foam as the stems bend easily, group together for more impact. Pennisetum will add a feathery softness to bridal bouquets and venue designs and is particularly suitable for autumn weddings. Coordinate with blues, peaches, dusky pinks and soft creams. Can be wired with care.

Pennisetum setaceum

For Students:

Family: Poaceae.

Genus & Species: *Pennisetum setaceum.*

Native to: Africa, Middle East, S/W Asia.

Trivia: Grown largely as an ornamental grass, although where it has been introduced into warmer climates such as Hawaii and South Africa, it has become an invasive weed.

Persicaria

Common Name: **Mountain fleece, Red bistort**

Availability: May–October.

Vase Life: 5–7 days.

Foliage Notes: A hardy perennial which grows in damp, moist soil. It changes from bright green in summer to red in the autumn. Tall stem length.

Colour Range: Bright green.

Conditioning:

- Ideal temperature range: 2–5°C (36–41°F).
- Hollow stemmed, cut with a sharp knife, leaving stem ends flat.
- Stand in clean, shallow water.
- Change water every 4–5 days.
- Store away from direct heat and draughts.

General Information:

- Don't overcrowd vases and containers, good ventilation is important.
- Suitable for using in both vase designs and floral foam.
- **Texture:** Ribbed.
- **Would complement:** Tropical flowers; Anthurium, Curcuma or Heliconia.

Persicaria amplexicaulis (Syn. *Polygonum amplexicaule*)

In Design and Wedding Work:
Interesting plant material which is excellent for constructions and for providing solid outlines to modern designs. It has a variety of uses, it can be sliced into small pieces and glued to cover large surfaces, or small pieces can be added into corsages and boutonnières. Individual segments can hold water, so it is possible to carve a hole into the stem to insert flowers or test tubes into. The same technique can be used to interlock stems together when constructing frames.
Foliage Meaning: Restoration.

For Students:
Family: Polygonaceae.
Genus & Species: *Persicaria* sp.
Native to: The Himalayas.
Trivia: Amplexicaulis comes partly from the work 'amplex' which means 'clasping the stem' a reference to the growth habit of the leaves.

Phalaenopsis

Common Name: **Moth orchid**

Availability: All year round.

Vase Life: 10–21 days.

Foliage Notes: Pronounced 'FAL-en-op-sis'. Orchid roots can be purchased as 'greenery' in their own right. Phalaenopsis and Vanda orchid roots are the most commonly available. Medium/long stem length.

Colour Range: Silvery grey-green.

Conditioning:

- Ideal temperature range: 2–5°C (36–41°F).
- If purchased in boxes keep in cold storage, dipping into when needed.
- Mist gently occasionally to keep up humidity.
- Store away from direct heat and draughts.

General Information:

- Orchid roots will gradually dry out becoming more brittle as they do so.
- Suitable for using in both vase designs and floral foam.
- **Texture:** Smooth.
- **Would complement:** Delicate spring flowers or tropical flowers and foliage.

Phalaenopsis amabilis

In Design and Wedding Work:

Excellent decorative material which has a variety of uses. Orchid roots can edge hand-tied posies, or reinforce a framework. In bridal designs a modern shower style can be accentuated and given a stylish edge with these silvery, delicate trails. Handle with care as roots can break if overstressed, keeping them slightly moist helps to overcome this problem. Mixed with other tropical greens they can create an exciting floral backdrop for corporate or competition work.

For Students:

Family: Orchidaceae.

Genus & Species: *Phalaenopsis* sp.

Native to: Tropical Asia.

Trivia: In their natural habitat Phalaenopsis grow on trees in tropical rainforests. They are epiphytic, a plant which grows on another without harming the host.

Philodendron

Availability: All year round.

Vase Life: 7–15 days.

Foliage Notes: A diverse group of evergreen plants which can be shrubs, trees or climbers. Their flowers are similar to arums, with green or reddish spathes. Medium stem length.

Colour Range: Dark glossy green.

Conditioning:

- Ideal temperature range: 12–15°C (54–59°F).
- Re-cut stems and stand in clean water, flower food is not necessary.
- Change water every 4–5 days.
- Store away from direct heat and draughts.

General Information:

- Long-lasting foliage suitable for using in both vase designs and floral foam.
- **Texture:** Smooth.
- **Leaf Shape:** Triangular/Pinnate.
- **Would complement:** Tropical flowers; Strelitzia, Anthurium or Protea.

Philodendron scandens

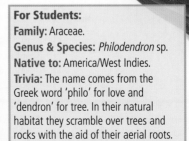

In Design and Wedding Work:

A useful leaf for modern and structured designs, Philodendron is robust and versatile. Use it to create a collar for a hand-tied or layer it to build up volume and texture. Philodendron will enhance focal interest in large arrangements where it would work with either traditional or more tropical materials. Not an obvious candidate for bridal work, although smaller leaves could be added into modern shower bouquets. Not suitable for wired work.

For Students:

Family: Araceae.

Genus & Species: *Philodendron* sp.

Native to: America/West Indies.

Trivia: The name comes from the Greek word 'philo' for love and 'dendron' for tree. In their natural habitat they scramble over trees and rocks with the aid of their aerial roots.

Phoenix

Common Name: **Pygmy date palm, Miniature date palm**

Availability: February–December.

Vase Life: 10–15 days.

Foliage Notes: An ornamental slow growing evergreen tree popular in the tropics. Small to medium in size, its edible fruits are not dissimilar to dates. Medium stem length.

Colour Range: Dark green.

Conditioning:

- Ideal temperature range: 12–15°C (54–59°F).
- Re-cut stems and stand in clean water, flower food is not necessary.
- Change water every 4–5 days.
- Store away from direct heat and draughts.

General Information:

- Long-lasting foliage suitable for using in both vase designs and floral foam.
- **Texture:** Feathery.
- **Leaf Shape:** Pinnate.
- **Would complement:** Showy flowers; lilies, Eremurus, Anthurium or orchid.

 x3 *Phoenix roebelenii*

In Design and Wedding Work:

A versatile leaf which has a multitude of uses in both modern and traditional designs. Phoenix is an inexpensive way to give the 'wow' factor to hand-tied bouquets and arrangements and will provide a strong, elegant outline to funeral tributes. Its leaflets can be plaited, woven and manipulated to give an extra flourish and are flexible enough to cascade and flow from designs. If looking for height, consider the Kentia palm (*Howea forsteriana*) which shares the same attributes, but is larger in size.

For Students:

Family: Arecaceae.

Genus & Species: *Phoenix roebelenii*.

Native to: South-eastern Asia.

Trivia: The distinctive fan like leaves of this attractive palm can have up to a hundred leaflets on each plane.

Phormium

Availability: All year round, scarce in August.

Vase Life: 10–15 days.

Foliage Notes: Pronounced 'For-me-um'. An evergreen perennial shrub which grows into large clumps of attractive sword-like leaves. Bears tall flower spikes in summer. Tall stem length.

Colour Range: Sage green with cream/pink/salmon/orange margins.

Conditioning:

- Ideal temperature range: 12–15°C (54–59°F).
- Re-cut stems with scissors or a sharp knife.
- Stand in tall containers in clean water with flower food.
- Change water every 4–5 days.
- Store away from direct heat and draughts.

General Information:

- Hardy, tough leaves that anchor well into floral foam.
- Browning edges can be trimmed for short term display.
- **Texture:** Smooth.
- **Leaf Shape:** Strap.
- **Would complement:** Tall flowers; lilies, Heliconia, gladioli, Helianthus.

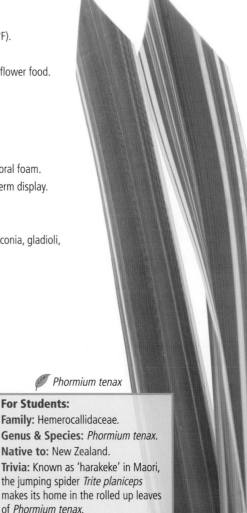

Phormium tenax

In Design and Wedding Work:

An obvious candidate for linear hand-tieds and arrangements, Phormium is very versatile; full height it will give drama and strong vertical lines, it is also robust enough to be rolled, pinned, woven and split. Use the strap-like leaves as part of a framework for large, ambitious structures. The attractive, finely striped variegation of Phormium will fit into most colour schemes, although its usefulness as a wedding foliage may be limited, it would not look out of place in large pedestal designs, and small pieces can be rolled and used in wired work.

For Students:

Family: Hemerocallidaceae.

Genus & Species: *Phormium tenax*.

Native to: New Zealand.

Trivia: Known as 'harakeke' in Maori, the jumping spider *Trite planiceps* makes its home in the rolled up leaves of *Phormium tenax*.

Photinia

Common Name: **Photinia, Red Robin**

Availability: August–December, peaks September–December.

Vase Life: 7–10 days.

Foliage Notes: Pronounced 'Foh-TIN-e-a'. A bushy evergreen with glossy leaves and small white flowers in summer followed by bright red berries in autumn. Medium stem length.

Colour Range: Mid-green and red.

Conditioning:

- Ideal temperature range: 2–5°C (36–41°F).
- Woody stemmed, re-cut with secateurs.
- Stand in clean water with flower food.
- Change water and re-cut stems every 3–4 days.
- Store away from direct heat and draughts.

General Information:

- Suitable for using in both vase designs and floral foam.
- Always ensure containers are kept topped up with water.
- **Texture:** Smooth/Glossy.
- **Leaf Shape:** Oval/Elliptic.
- **Would complement:** Autumnal flowers and colours.

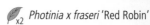 *Photinia x fraseri* 'Red Robin'

In Design and Wedding Work:

Large boughs of Photinia would look fantastic in pedestal arrangements where height and drama are required. Bright and distinctive it works beautifully with strong colour schemes and particularly suits natural, garden style designs. Perhaps too bushy for modern schemes, it can however be added into vases and won't look out of place in natural hand-tied posies. Individual leaves are suitable for wiring.

For Students:

Family: Rosaceae.

Genus & Species: *Photinia x fraseri.*

Native to: Himalayas & Asia.

Trivia: Photinia produces bright red berries in large quantities, which are very popular with birds such as thrushes and starlings, who in return for the feast, help to spread the seed.

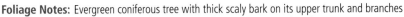

Availability: November–December.

Vase Life: 10–21 days.

Foliage Notes: Evergreen coniferous tree with thick scaly bark on its upper trunk and branches with soft whorls of aromatic needles. Medium stem length.

Colour Range: Dark green.

Conditioning:

- Ideal temperature range: 2–5°C (36–41°F).
- Sold in bundles which can be stored outside until needed.
- Woody stemmed. Remove foliage in contact with water.
- Change water every 4–5 days.
- Store away from direct heat and draughts.

Pinus sylvestris

General Information:

- Exudes a sticky sap which can stain fingers.
- Long-lasting foliage suitable for using in both vase designs and floral foam.
- **Texture:** Bushy.
- **Leaf Shape:** Needle.
- **Would complement:** Christmas flowers and foliage.

In Design and Wedding Work:

Lovely seasonal foliage which can be used in a wide range of Christmas designs, add into garlands and swags, door wreaths and table arrangements. Pinus is quite pliable so is easy to manipulate and is great for textured designs. Aromatic and attractive it is good value for money, long-lasting and robust. In bridal work pieces of pine can be added into natural tied posies, but beware of its sticky sap which is its biggest drawback. For this reason, not suitable for wiring.

For Students:

Family: Pinaceae.

Genus & Species: *Pinus* sp.

Native to: Europe & Asia.

Trivia: Capable of growing up to 46m (138'), the oldest recorded specimens of Scots pine are in Scandinavia and are over 700 years old.

Pistacia

Common Name: **Pistacia**

Availability: All year round, scarce in July.

Vase Life: 10–14 days.

Foliage Notes: Pronounced 'pis-TACH-e-a'. A member of the Cashew family, these small trees are hardy and tough, preferring dry, Mediterranean style conditions. Medium stem length.

Colour Range: Lawn green.

Conditioning:

- Ideal temperature range: 2–5°C (36–41°F).
- Woody stemmed, re-cut with secateurs.
- Stand in clean water with flower food.
- Change water every 4–5 days.
- Store away from direct heat and draughts.

General Information:

- Long-lasting foliage suitable for using in both vase designs and floral foam.
- Beware of the sticky resin.
- **Texture:** Bushy.
- **Leaf Shape:** Pinnate.
- **Would complement:** Small, delicate flowers such as spray roses, Ranunculus or scabious.

In Design and Wedding Work:
Pistacia is an attractive, study, erect foliage with delicate leaflets which naturally lends itself to smaller designs. Spring flowers would work particularly well with this foliage, either arranged as small posies or in vases. As it's quite bushy, it's excellent for filling out hand-tieds and arrangements and for foliage edging tributes. It will add texture to garlands and wall swags and small pieces can be used in wired designs although beware of its sticky resin.

 Pistacia lentiscus

For Students:
Family: Anacardiaceae.
Genus & Species: *Pistacia lentiscus.*
Native to: Mediterranean regions.
Trivia: Most famous in the genus is *P. vera* from where the pistachio nut comes from. Slow growing, the trees only bear fruit after a number of years.

Pittosporum

Availability: All year round.

Vase Life: 7–10 days.

Foliage Notes: Pronounced 'Pit-o-SPOOR-um'. Evergreen shrubs with attractive foliage. Fragrant flowers in summer are followed by seeds coated with a sticky resin in autumn. Medium stem length.

Colour Range: Light green with cream margins.

Conditioning:

- Ideal temperature range: 2–5°C (36–41°F).
- Woody stemmed, re-cut and stand in clean, fresh water.
- Change water every 4–5 days.
- Store away from direct heat and draughts.

General Information:

- Long-lasting foliage suitable for using in both vase designs and floral foam.
- **Texture:** Bushy.
- **Leaf Shape:** Oval/Elliptic.
- **Would complement:** Traditional, unfussy flowers.

Pittosporum tenuifolium

Pittosporum tobira 'Variegatum'

In Design and Wedding Work:
A very useful and versatile foliage which has become a staple in many florists' workrooms. The smaller leaved *P. tenuifolium* is lovely for adding into hand-tieds, particularly with delicate spring and summer flowers and is very useful for foliage edged tributes. Small pieces of it can also be included in wired bridal work. The larger leaved *P. tobira* is not as attractive, but is good value for money, particularly in large pedestal arrangements and funeral sprays where its variegated foliage will add contrast.

For Students:
Family: Pittosporaceae.
Genus & Species: *Pittosporum* sp.
Native to: Australia, S. Africa, E. Asia.
Trivia: The sticky resin which coats the seeds of pittosporum is the clue to where the name comes from, in Ancient Greek it means 'pitch-seed'.

109

Plagiothecium

Common Name: **Flat moss, Waved silk-moss**

Availability: All year round.

Vase Life: 15–30 days.

Foliage Notes: Pronounced 'Play-jee-oh-THEE-see-um'. A conspicuous moss with flattened shoots that have tiny wavy leaves no bigger than 3mm long. Medium stem length.

Colour Range: Pale green.

Conditioning:

- Ideal temperature range: 2–5°C (36–41°F).
- Store in a refrigerated room for maximum life.
- Leave moss in the polystyrene box it arrives in and use as necessary.
- Store away from direct heat and draughts.

General Information:

- Long-lasting, suitable for using in planted designs and arrangements.
- Mist occasionally with water to keep it fresh.
- **Texture:** Rough.
- **Would complement:** Spring flowers, planted bowls, vegetative arrangements.

In Design and Wedding Work:

An extremely versatile moss which no workroom should be without. In its most basic form use flat moss to cover compost in planted designs, it will also complement spring bulbs and Easter planted gardens. This moss is also excellent for textured designs, whether as floral gifts or for funeral tributes where it is also suitable as a basing material. In contemporary wedding work use it as a natural covering for bridal holders. Moss spheres can be made by rolling and then binding moss with wire.

Plagiothecium undulatum

For Students:

Family: Plagiotheciaceae.

Genus & Species: *Plagiothecium undulatum.*

Native to: Great Britain.

Trivia: Found in deciduous woodland and conifer plantations, Plagiothecium can also often be found growing amongst boulders and in blanket bogs.

Platycerium

Availability: All year round.

Vase Life: 10–14 days.

Foliage Notes: Pronounced 'Plat-e-SIR-ee-rum'. An evergreen epiphytic fern with kidney shaped basal fronds that are in stark contrast to the spectacular, antler-like fronds above. Short stem length.

Colour Range: Sage green with a silvery sheen.

Conditioning:

- Ideal temperature range: 12–15°C (54–59°F).
- If using a plant stand in semi-shade, out of direct sunlight.
- Keep compost moist and mist regularly.

General Information:

- Rarely available as a cut foliage, invest in a plant instead.
- Suitable for using in floral foam.
- **Texture:** Furry/Smooth.
- **Leaf Shape:** Forked, varying in form.
- **Would complement:** Delicate, textural flowers; Ranunculus, Muscari, or Hellebore

In Design and Wedding Work:

Platycerium is fascinating foliage superb for textured, contemporary designs. As it doesn't have a stem, it's not really suitable for vases, but can be used very effectively in vegetative arrangements and would look lovely in spring designs where its silvery sheen would complement crisp whites and greens. Despite its unconventional appearance it can be used in bridal designs where it will sit alongside similarly natural materials arranged in limited bouquets on holders.

 x2 *Platycerium bifurcatum*

For Students:

Family: Polypodiaceae.

Genus & Species: *Platycerium bifurcatum.*

Native to: Asia & Australia.

Trivia: Mature Staghorns can grow more than 1m wide; it is possible to propagate them by strapping cuttings to trees where they take root in the bark.

Prunus

Common Name: **Japanese flowering cherry**

Availability: March–May.

Vase Life: 3–5 days.

Foliage Notes: Flowering cherry has pretty, delicate flowers in spring and attractive autumn colour. Ornamental cherry fruits are edible but not overly tasty. Medium/tall stem length.

Colour Range: Pale pink to creamy white.

Conditioning:

- Ideal temperature range: 2–5°C (36–41°F).
- Woody stemmed, re-cut with secateurs.
- Stand in clean water with flower food and keep containers topped up.
- Change water every 2–3 days.
- Store away from direct heat and draughts.

General Information:

- Once cut, stems are short-lived, so more suitable for vase designs than floral foam.
- Handle with care as buds can be knocked off easily.
- Don't mist stems as this can mark flowers.
- **Leaf Shape:** Oval.
- **Would complement:** Seasonal spring flowers such as Fritillaria, Ranunculus or Moluccella.

In Design and Wedding Work:
Bring spring inside with boughs of fragrant, pretty cherry blossom. Once cut the flowers can be short-lived so not recommended for designs that need to be in situ for a while, but perfect for weddings and for creating instant impact. Its woody stem means that it is better in vases than in floral foam, but if using in foam make sure containers are kept well topped up. Large lengths of cherry blossom would look beautiful in marquee weddings and are perfect for decorating archways.

 x3 *Prunus amanogawa*

For Students:
Family: Rosaceae.
Genus & Species: *Prunus* sp.
Native to: Northern temperate zones.
Trivia: The Prunus genus is huge, over 400 species and includes cherry, peach, nectarine, almond and plum.

Prunus

Availability: July–April, peaks September to March.

Vase Life: 14–21 days.

Foliage Notes: A vigorous evergreen shrub with erect racemes of small white flowers in summer followed by bright red berries. Sometimes grown as a hedge. Medium stem length.

Colour Range: Dark glossy green.

Conditioning:

- Ideal temperature range: 2–5°C (36–41°F).
- Woody stemmed, re-cut with secateurs.
- Stand in clean water, flower food is not necessary.
- Change water every 4–5 days.
- Store away from direct heat and draughts.

General Information:

- Long-lasting foliage suitable for using in both vase designs and floral foam.
- **Texture:** Smooth/Shiny.
- **Leaf Shape:** Elliptic.
- **Would complement:** Traditional flowers such as Chrysanthemum, lilies and Alstroemeria.

×3 *Prunus laurocerasus*

In Design and Wedding Work:
Laurel is indispensable when you need height and volume for large pedestal and venue designs and as it is common in gardens, it is an inexpensive way to fill out arrangements. Individual leaves are flexible enough to be rolled and pinned or used as a basing material such as in the construction of chaplets. Useful for funeral sprays, but use sparingly as it can overpower other flowers and foliages.
Foliage Meaning: Glory.

For Students:
Family: Rosaceae.
Genus & Species: *Prunus laurocerasus.*
Native to: E. Europe & S.W. Asia.
Trivia: Although Common Laurel is used for making laurel chaplets it should not be confused with *Laurus nobilis* (Bay).

113

Quercus

Common Name: **Oak**

Availability: August–November, peaks September–October.

Vase Life: 5–7 days.

Foliage Notes: Deciduous or evergreen trees with inconspicuous flowers in spring followed by attractive acorns in autumn along with great seasonal colour. Medium/tall stem length.

Colour Range: Moss green to rich burgundy.

Conditioning:

- Ideal temperature range: 2–5°C (36–41°F).
- Woody stemmed, re-cut and stand in clean water with flower food.
- Change water every 2–3 days.
- Store away from direct heat and draughts.

Quercus palustris

General Information:

- Will dry out quickly if left out of water or in a warm room.
- Suitable for using in both vase designs and floral foam.
- **Texture:** Smooth.
- **Leaf Shape:** Obovate with deep lobes.
- **Would complement:** Autumn flowers such as Carthamus, Helianthus and gladioli.

 *Quercus rubra*

In Design and Wedding Work:

The fact that this colourful, attractive foliage is only available for a short time simply adds to its seasonal appeal. Long lengths of oak will complement arrangements and vase designs in both traditional and contemporary styles, although be careful using in contract work as it dries out in warm temperatures. It will look stunning in hand-ties and bridal work where a seasonal theme has been chosen. Dried oak leaves look great scattered along tables. Can be wired with care.

Foliage Meaning: Bravery.

For Students:

Family: Fagaceae.

Genus & Species: *Quercus* sp.

Native to: Northern hemisphere.

Trivia: The Couch Oak in Addlestone, Surrey, is reputed to have originated in the 11th Century, local legend says that Elizabeth I had a picnic beneath its boughs.

Rhapis

Common Name: **Rhapis, Lady palm, Finger palm**

Availability: All year round.

Vase Life: 10–15 days.

Foliage Notes: Rhapis grow in multi-stemmed upright clumps up to 4m (12') and bear fleshy, white fruits; it propagates via offshoots from underground rhizomes. Medium stem length.

Colour Range: Green.

Conditioning:

- Ideal temperature range: 12–15°C (54–59°F).
- Re-cut stems at an angle, preferably with a sharp knife.
- Stand in clean water with flower food.
- Change water every 4–5 days.
- Store away from direct heat sources and draughts.

General Information:

- Brown ends of leaves can be trimmed off.
- Long-lasting foliage suitable for using in both vase designs and floral foam.
- **Texture:** Smooth/Glossy.
- **Leaf Shape:** Palmate.
- **Would complement:** Tropical flowers; Curcuma, Anthurium, Strelitzia.

 Rhapis excelsa

In Design and Wedding Work:
Distinctive foliage, reliable and robust whose strong lines are ideal for structured, contemporary design. Use Rhapis to give a defining outline to funeral sprays and modern pedestal arrangements; it will also make an interesting collar for hand-tieds and is a great focal foliage. Fronds can be trimmed without damage, so it is possible to create some interesting shapes from these striking leaves.

For Students:
Family: Arecaceae.

Genus & Species: *Rhapis excelsa*.

Native to: S. China & Taiwan.

Trivia: A popular houseplant, Rhapis can often be found in office landscaping schemes or shopping malls as it is relatively tolerant of cold and exposure.

115

Rhipsalis

Common Name: **Rhipsalis, Mistletoe cactus**

Availability: All year round.

Vase Life: 7–12 days.

Foliage Notes: A succulent, epiphytic forest cacti with a trailing habit that attaches itself to trees in its natural environment. Small green fruits turn white as they mature. Medium/tall stem length.

Colour Range: Bright green.

Conditioning:

- Ideal temperature range: 2–5°C (36–41°F).
- If using a plant, keep it in a well-lit spot, shaded from direct sunlight.
- Mist frequently.
- Compost should be moist but not over wet.

General Information:

- Rhipsalis is quite brittle, handle with care.
- Suitable for using in both vase designs and floral foam.
- **Texture:** Spiky.
- **Would complement:** Small, delicate flowers; Hellebore, Muscari or Ranunculus.

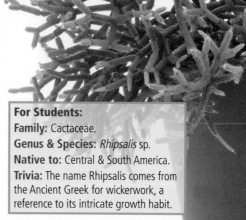

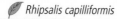 *Rhipsalis capilliformis*

In Design and Wedding Work:
Rhipsalis is a choice foliage and not one commonly available commercially. The easiest way to obtain it to use it in design work is to take cuttings from plants. Generally not strong enough to use unsupported in floral foam, wiring is the safest option. Hugely effective in delicate, modern designs, trial it from the tops of vases or use it for additional texture. In weddings, it would work beautifully in modern cascade bouquets. Not suitable for buttonholes or corsages.

For Students:
Family: Cactaceae.
Genus & Species: *Rhipsalis* sp.
Native to: Central & South America.
Trivia: The name Rhipsalis comes from the Ancient Greek for wickerwork, a reference to its intricate growth habit.

Rhododendron

Common Name: **Rhododendron, Rhodos**

Availability: All year round.

Vase Life: 12–21 days.

Foliage Notes: Bushy evergreen or deciduous shrub with colourful, showy, trumpet shaped flowers in spring, commonly found in woodland and parks. Tall stem length.

Colour Range: Dark green with contrasting undersides of leaves.

Conditioning:

- Ideal temperature range: 2–5°C (36–41°F).
- Re-cut stems, preferably with secateurs.
- Stand in clean water with flower food.
- Change water every 4–5 days.
- Store away from direct heat and draughts.

General Information:

- Hardy, tough leaves with a woody stem.
- Long-lasting foliage suitable for using in both vase designs and floral foam.
- **Texture:** Smooth/Glossy.
- **Leaf Shape:** Oblong.
- **Would complement:** Traditional flowers; Chrysanthemums, lilies or carnations.

In Design and Wedding Work:

Stems of Rhododendron are fantastic for large pedestal arrangements, indeed anywhere that big, showy statements are required. Conversely, individual leaves of this robust shrub can be wired, rolled and pinned and used in textured design work, with the brown, downy underside giving an interesting contrast to its glossy green upper. In wedding work the leaves can be used to base bridal holders or to create drama and impact in reception and venue designs.

Foliage Meaning: Danger, beware.

Rhododendron ponticum ×2

For Students:

Family: Ericaceae.

Genus & Species: *Rhododendron* sp.

Native to: Asia, Europe & N. America.

Trivia: An incredibly diverse group of plants ranging in size from tiny alpine species up to *R. giganteum* which can grow up to 30m (98') tall.

117

Rosa

Common Name: **Rose hips, Rose haw**

Availability: August–December, peaks September–November.

Vase Life: 5–10 days.

Foliage Notes: Distinctive, fleshy fruit which starts to ripen in late summer/autumn. They vary in shape and size from round to bottle shaped. Medium stem length.

Colour Range: Red/orange to purple/black.

Conditioning:

- Ideal temperature range: 2–5°C (36–41°F).
- Re-cut stems, preferably with secateurs, handling with care.
- Stand in clean water with flower food.
- Change water every 2–3 days.
- Store away from direct heat and draughts which will cause hips to wither.

General Information:

- Commercial varieties are available and many are thorn free!
- Remove excess foliage from stems.
- Suitable for using in both vase designs and floral foam.
- **Texture:** Smooth.
- **Would complement:** Dahlia, Papaver, spray roses or Crocosmia.

Rosa xanthine 'Canary Bird'

In Design and Wedding Work:

Perfect for adding essential seasonal accents to autumn designs and funeral tributes; include in tied posies and hand-tied bouquets also traditional and modern arrangements in floral foam. Lovely for informal bridal work where rose hips would be equally effective in both contemporary and more traditional designs. Can be wired with care, but don't cut or split the hips as the hairs inside cause intense irritation.

For Students:

Family: Rosaceae.

Genus & Species: *Rosa* sp.

Native to: Northern hemisphere.

Trivia: The uses for rose hips are varied and wide ranging; they can be eaten, drunk or dried and are an excellent source of vitamin C for both humans and animals.

Rosmarinus

Common Name: **Rosemary**

Availability: October–February, also May.

Vase Life: 7–14 days.

Foliage Notes: A popular evergreen herb, aromatic and fragrant, rosemary bears pretty two lipped blue flowers borne in small clusters in early summer. Medium stem length.

Colour Range: Grey-green.

Conditioning:

- Ideal temperature range: 2–5°C (36–41°F).
- Re-cut stems and remove any foliage in contact with water.
- Woody stemmed, stand in clean water with flower food.
- Change water every 4–5 days.
- Store away from direct heat and draughts.

General Information:

- Although a culinary herb, avoid eating rosemary commercially grown for cut flower use.
- Suitable for using in both vase designs and floral foam.
- **Texture:** Bushy.
- **Leaf Shape:** Needle.
- **Would complement:** Delicate flowers; Alchemilla, Bouvardia, Freesia or Astrantia.

Rosmarinus officinalis

In Design and Wedding Work:

Scented rosemary would be a lovely addition to natural hand-tied posies and seasonal arrangements, where its delicate foliage and upright habit would be a foil to more colourful and flamboyant flowers. As rosemary stands for remembrance it would be a thoughtful gesture to include it in funeral tributes. In wedding work use in bridal posies and venue designs, although its short stems wouldn't be suitable for large pedestals. It can also be used in wired work.

For Students:

Family: Lamiaceae.

Genus & Species: *Rosmarinus officinalis*.

Native to: Mediterranean.

Trivia: Rosmarinus comes from the Latin 'ros' dew and 'marinus' sea, i.e. dew of the sea; as it was believed that the humidity created by sea breezes was all that was needed to keep it alive.

Rubus

Common Name: **Blackberry, Bramble**

Availability: June–October, peaks June–August.

Vase Life: 5–8 days.

Foliage Notes: A bushy, prickly perennial with white or pink flowers in summer followed by juicy edible fruit. Often viewed as an unwelcome garden guest. Short stem length.

Colour Range: Fruits range from green to dark red.

Conditioning:

- Ideal temperature range: 2–5°C (36–41°F).
- Re-cut stems, preferably with secateurs, handling with care.
- Stand in clean water with flower food.
- Change water every 2–3 days and store away from direct heat and draughts.

General Information:

- Do not be tempted to eat Rubus commercially grown for the cut flower market.
- Avoid spraying fruits as this can encourage mould.
- Commercial varieties have been developed which are prickle free.
- **Texture:** Globular.
- **Would complement:** Small, seasonal flowers; oregano, Helenium or Hypericum.

 Rubus fruticosus

In Design and Wedding Work:
Essential for late summer/early autumn design work where seasonality is key. Blackberries would look simply gorgeous in natural hand-tied posies and simple vase designs. It can be used in floral foam, but may get a little overpowered in large arrangements. Resist the temptation to use garden grown blackberries in bridal work because of its prickles and in case of staining. Can be wired with care.
Foliage meaning: Remorse, envy.

For Students:
Family: Rosaceae.
Genus & Species: *Rubus fruticosus.*
Native to: Temperate N. hemisphere.
Trivia: Blackberries were found in the stomach contents of Haraldskaer Woman, a bog body found in Jutland, Denmark dating from the 5th Century BC.

Rubus

Common Name: **Chinese bramble, Creeping bramble**

Availability: June–October.

Vase Life: 10–14 days.

Foliage Notes: A vigorous and attractive shrub which provides excellent ground cover. Easy to grow, it is often seen as part of commercial or local authority planting schemes. Medium/tall stem length.

Colour Range: Dark green with a furry red stem.

Conditioning:

- Ideal temperature range: 2–5°C (36–41°F).
- Re-cut stems, handling with care as it can become easily tangled.
- Stand in clean water with flower food.
- Change water every 4–5 days.
- Store away from direct heat and draughts.

General Information:

- Hard to come by commercially, this is a shrub to cultivate in your garden.
- Long-lasting and suitable for using in both vase designs and floral foam.
- **Texture:** Bristly.
- **Leaf Shape:** Heart.
- **Would complement:** Natural garden flowers, especially with an autumn feel.

In Design and Wedding Work:

R. tricolour is ideal for adding volume to large arrangements at little cost. Its long lengths trial beautifully and it is flexible enough to wrap around hand-ties to create a natural collar or to scramble through structures and frameworks. It is lovely in seasonal summer and autumn bridal designs where it will look equally effective cascading from an ornate shower bouquet as it will tumbling from tall vases. Mature leaves can be wired with care.

 Rubus tricolour

For Students:

Family: Rosaceae.

Genus & Species: *Rubus tricolour.*

Native to: Western China.

Trivia: Occurring naturally on steep banks and mountain sides, *R. tricolour* can be found at altitudes up to 3,000m.

121

Ruscus

Availability: All year round.

Vase Life: 15–30 days.

Foliage Notes: A slow growing evergreen bush with tall, erect stems. Robust and glossy, it bears insignificant white flowers in spring. Medium stem length.

Colour Range: Dark green.

Conditioning:

- Ideal temperature range: 2–5°C (36–41°F).
- Re-cut stems and stand in clean water with flower food.
- Change water every 4–5 days.
- Store away from direct heat and draughts.

General Information:

- Ruscus painted gold and silver is often available at Christmas time.
- Long-lasting foliage suitable for using in both vase designs and floral foam.
- **Texture:** Smooth.
- **Leaf Shape:** Oval.
- **Would complement:** Traditional flowers such as carnations, Alstroemeria, lisianthus or Freesia.

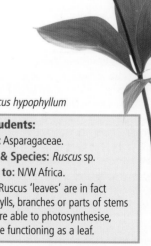

In Design and Wedding Work:
Extremely popular foliage, with a multitude of uses. Its straight form and regular appearance make Ruscus a reliable filler for hand-tied bouquets, funeral sprays and arrangements. Cut into small sections it is very useful for filling in 'holes' in designs in floral foam and for edging tributes. Individual 'leaves' are tough enough to be rolled and pinned and are often used in buttonholes and corsages. Good value and extremely long-lasting.

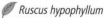 *Ruscus hypophyllum*

For Students:
Family: Asparagaceae.
Genus & Species: *Ruscus* sp.
Native to: N/W Africa.
Trivia: Ruscus 'leaves' are in fact cladophylls, branches or parts of stems which are able to photosynthesise, therefore functioning as a leaf.

Salix

Common Name: **Twisted willow, Corkscrew willow**

Availability: All year, peaks September–March.

Vase Life: 10–30 days.

Foliage Notes: A very distinctive tree with slim, upright growth and twisted branches that are used extensively in floristry and decorative work. Produces catkins in early spring. Tall stem length.

Colour Range: Fresh green maturing to orange/gold.

Conditioning:

- Ideal temperature range: 2–5°C (36–41°F).
- Re-cut with secateurs; try not to tangle stems!
- Stand in clean water, flower food is not necessary.
- Change water every 4–5 days.
- Store away from direct heat and draughts.

General Information:

- Fresh cut Salix will continue to root and sprout leaves, all off which can be trimmed off.
- Woody stemmed, Salix will dry out and become brittle the longer it is stored.
- **Texture:** Smooth.
- **Shape:** Corkscrew.
- **Would complement:** Tall flowers; lilies, Strelitzia or Heliconia.

In Design and Wedding Work:

Twisted willow will add instant height and drama to modern designs and it wouldn't look out of place in more traditional arrangements either. Use it to form the base of frameworks and structures, although only its main stem is strong enough to take any real weight. It is quite flexible, particularly when fresh, and can be bent and curved with care. Test tubes and decorative materials can be hung from its twisted branches. Small sections can used in wired work.

 Salix babylonica 'Tortuosa'

For Students:

Family: Salicaceae.

Genus & Species: *Salix babylonica.*

Native to: N. China.

Trivia: *Salix* 'Tortuosa' is thought to have spread to the west from China along the silk route, a trade corridor which extended 4,000 miles into Africa and Europe.

Salix

Common Name: **Pussy willow, Florist's willow, Goat willow**

Availability: October–May, peaks November–April.

Vase Life: 5–7 days.

Foliage Notes: A pretty, deciduous ornamental tree with a rounded appearance. It has soft, furry catkins which appear in spring. Medium/tall stem length.

Colour Range: Chocolate brown bark with silver-grey catkins.

Conditioning:

- Ideal temperature range: 2–5°C (36–41°F).
- Woody stemmed; re-cut with secateurs, handling with care.
- Stand in clean water with flower food.
- Change water every 2–3 days.
- Store away from direct heat and draughts.

General Information:

- As pussy willow matures, yellow pollen will develop on the catkins.
- Avoid catkins touching water and don't overcrowd buckets.
- **Texture:** Smooth/Furry.
- **Shape:** Linear.
- **Would complement:** Spring flowers including Ranunculus, Moluccella and Anemone.

In Design and Wedding Work:

Truly seasonal, pussy willow is also very versatile. Available in both short and tall lengths use it at full height to add structure and line to designs, it is also malleable enough to bend and curve when fresh. Incorporate into spring hand-tieds, either in straight pieces or looped to create an interesting collar effect. In bridal work it will give instant seasonality to natural tied posies and would be lovely in informal reception and venue arrangements. Can be wired with care.

Salix caprea

For Students:

Family: Salicaceae.

Genus & Species: *Salix caprea*.

Native to: United Kingdom.

Trivia: One of the earliest signs of spring, pussy willow is a favourite flower for Chinese New Year where it is seen as a symbol of prosperity.

Salvia

Availability: May–October.

Vase Life: 5–7 days.

Foliage Notes: A bushy, spreading, aromatic herb, popular in cooking, which bears small spikes of pretty, pale blue flowers in early summer. Medium stem length.

Colour Range: Grey-green.

Conditioning:

- Ideal temperature range: 2–5°C (36–41°F).
- Re-cut stems and place immediately in fresh water with flower food.
- Change water every 2–3 days, re-cutting stems each time.
- Store away from direct heat and draughts.

General Information:

- The flowers of non-commercially grown sage drop easily.
- Suitable for using in both vase designs and floral foam.
- **Texture:** Bushy.
- **Leaf Shape:** Oblong.
- **Would complement:** Pretty summer flowers; scabious, lavender or Bouvardia.

Salvia officinalis

In Design and Wedding Work:
A lovely foliage for hand-tied bouquets and simple vase designs, although its aromatic scent could be a little overpowering in a warm room or marquee. Perfect for summer weddings, especially when combined with natural garden flowers and herbs. Salvia will last longer in vase designs than in floral foam; always ensure containers are kept topped up with water. Can be added into natural tied bridal posies, although it is a little too soft for wiring.

Foliage meaning: Virtue.

For Students:
Family: Lamiaceae.

Genus & Species: *Salvia officinalis.*

Native to: Mediterranean.

Trivia: Sage has many uses in herbal medicine as well as in the kitchen. Sage tea is popular for soothing sore throats, and fresh sage can be used as a compress on cuts and wounds.

125

Schoenus

Common Name: **Flexigrass**

Availability: All year round.

Vase Life: 14–21 days.

Foliage Notes: Pronounced 'SHOW-nus'. A strong, tubular grass approximately 1–2mm in diameter. Sold in weighted bunches between 50–60 stems per bunch. Tall stem length.

Colour Range: Mid/light green.

Conditioning:

- Ideal temperature range: 2–5°C (36–41°F).
- Re-cut stems, preferably with scissors.
- Stand in clean, fresh water, flower food is not necessary.
- Change water every 4–5 days.
- Store away from direct heat and draughts.

General Information:

- If delivered in plastic, leave it on, as it helps to keep it in check!
- Long-lasting and suitable for using in both vase designs and floral foam.
- **Texture:** Smooth.
- **Would complement:** Tall, sculptural flowers such as Hippeastrum, Strelitzia or Eremurus

In Design and Wedding Work:

Flexigrass certainly lives up to its name as it is malleable enough to bend without snapping or forming unwanted angles. It has a multitude of uses in design work, giving subtle movement to arrangements, linking floral elements together and adding valuable extra space and dimension for very little cost. Flexigrass can also be bound, plaited or knotted, all in all, great fun to use. In weddings, add flexigrass into wired work for a bit of extra pizazz.

 Schoenus melanostachys

For Students:

Family: Cyperaceae.

Genus & Species: *Schoenus melanostachys.*

Native to: South Africa.

Trivia: Schoenus is a sedge – not to be confused with a grass or a rush! There are over 5,500 species of sedge widely distributed across the globe.

Common Name: **Ice plant, Showy stonecrop**

Availability: June–October.

Vase Life: 7–10 days.

Foliage Notes: A popular garden shrub, Sedum is an attractive succulent with fleshy leaves and flat flower heads. Medium stem length.

Colour Range: Lawn green maturing to burgundy.

Conditioning:

- Ideal temperature range: 5–8°C (41–46°F).
- Re-cut stems and stand in clean water with flower food.
- Remove any foliage in contact with water.
- Change water every 4–5 days.
- Store away from direct heat and draughts.

General Information:

- If using straight from the garden, condition overnight first.
- Long-lasting foliage suitable for using in both vase designs and floral foam.
- **Texture:** Rough.
- **Leaf Shape:** Ovate.
- **Would complement:** Small headed flowers, scabious, Ornithogalum or Callistephus.

Sedum spectabile

In Design and Wedding Work:

The fresh green of Sedum is a lovely contrast to both vibrant and more subtle colour schemes. Bordering between foliage and flower, Sedum is perfectly at home in natural tied posies, traditional or modern designs and vase arrangements – it is very versatile! Solid and dependable, it is excellent for textured work, although it lacks natural movement. Small pieces of Sedum can be used effectively in wired designs.

Foliage meaning: Your looks freeze me.

For Students:

Family: Crassulaceae.

Genus & Species: *Sedum spectabile.*

Native to: Eastern Asia.

Trivia: The Sedum Society is an organisation dedicated to preserving as many species of Sedum as possible. They operate a Sedum exchange scheme and publish a quarterly newsletter.

Senecio

Common Name: **Silver ragwort, Dusty miller**

Availability: May–September.

Vase Life: 7–10 days.

Foliage Notes: Pronounced 'Sen-EK-e-o'. A popular summer bedding plant, hardy and tougher than it looks, capable of surviving even some of the coldest winters. Medium stem length.

Colour Range: Pale silver-grey.

Conditioning:

- Ideal temperature range: 2–5°C (36–41°F).
- Re-cut stems and release from bunches, taking care not to overcrowd containers.
- Stand in clean water with flower food.
- Change water every 4–5 days.
- Store away from direct heat and draughts.

General Information:

- Senecio need good air circulation, also any foliage touching water should be removed.
- Long-lasting, suitable for using in both vase designs and floral foam.
- **Texture:** Furry.
- **Leaf Shape:** Pinnate.
- **Would complement:** Pretty summer flowers; Nigella, Ageratum, Astilbe or Echinops.

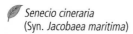
Senecio cineraria
(Syn. *Jacobaea maritima*)

In Design and Wedding Work:
Senecio's delicate silver foliage is a welcome alternative to green in the summer; use it to lift colour schemes where it would work particularly well with blue, dusky pink and cream. Stems are strong enough for using in floral foam, include it in both traditional and contemporary designs. Combine into natural hand-tied posies with grasses and seed heads for a truly country look. Would suit all areas of bridal work; leaves can be wired with care.

For Students:
Family: Asteraceae.
Genus & Species: *Senecio cineraria*.
Native to: Mediterranean regions.
Trivia: Senecio's ability to tolerate salt, plus its resistance to fire and deer make it a popular garden plant in states on the west coast of America.

Senecio

Availability: All year round.

Vase Life: 10–15 days.

Foliage Notes: An attractive succulent with long, pendant stems which bear elongated, bead-like leaves. Has tiny, compound flowers composed of many florets. Medium stem length.

Colour Range: Bright green.

Conditioning:

- Ideal temperature range: 10–13°C (50–55°F).
- If using a plant, stand it in a sunny position with some shade from direct sunlight.
- Water thoroughly when compost dries out.
- Senecio appreciates fresh air, open windows in summer.

General Information:

- Keep plants suspended to prevent tangling and damage, cut when needed.
- Suitable for using in both vase designs and floral foam.
- **Texture:** Globular.
- **Leaf Shape:** Elliptical.
- **Would complement:** Small, ornate flowers; Ornithogalum, Eucharis lily, Dendrobium.

In Design and Wedding Work:

A delicate and interesting foliage which works best in contemporary work where its form can be appreciated. Trail from bridal cascade bouquets with similar types of foliage such as Ceropegia to provide contrast. A little too delicate to wire flowers onto unless they are very light, it can be looped, threaded and wound through arrangements and designs. Use it in wired work where it is particularly effective in floral jewellery and designs created for body adornment.

Senecio herrianus

For Students:

Family: Asteraceae.

Genus & Species: *Senecio herrianus.*

Native to: Namibia.

Trivia: Despite its delicate appearance, *S. herrianus* can withstand temperatures down to -6°C (21°F). It was first described in 1932 by German botanist Moritz Kurt Dinter.

129

Setaria

Common Name: **Foxtail millet**

Availability: April–December, peaks May–October.

Vase Life: 5–10 days.

Foliage Notes: Pronounced 'Set-AR-rea'. An annual grass with a dense, hairy seed head resembling a miniature fox tail, hence its common name. Medium stem length.

Colour Range: Pale green with red tinges.

Conditioning:

- Ideal temperature range: 2–5°C (36–41°F).
- Re-cut stems with scissors, removing any loose leaves.
- Stand in clean water with flower food.
- Change water every 3–4 days.
- Store away from direct heat and draughts.

General Information:

- Can snap easily, handle with care.
- Grown for its seed head, any marked or damaged leaves can be removed.
- **Texture:** Bristly.
- **Leaf Shape:** Linear.
- **Would complement:** Summer flowers; Nigella, scabious, cornflower or Helenium.

 Setaria italica

In Design and Wedding Work:
Perfect for summer styling, add Setaria into natural tied posies and textured designs or tributes. Simple, rustic arrangements will be ideal for this attractive grass. Most effective when used in groups rather than singly, strip off any unsightly leaves. Setaria is bold and strong enough to include in large pedestal designs, although care should be taken when inserting it into floral foam, as the stem can bend easily. Can be wired if handled gently.

For Students:
Family: Poaceae.
Genus & Species: *Setaria italica.*
Native to: Europe, Asia and Africa.
Trivia: Setaria is the second most widely planted species of millet in the world, and has been grown in China since the sixth century BC.

Sphagnum

Common Name: **Sphagnum moss, Bog moss, Peat moss**

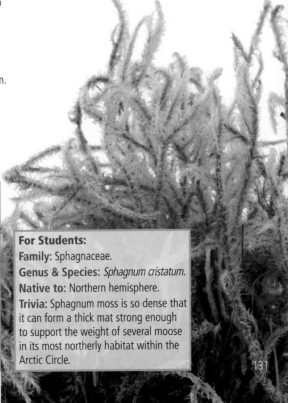

Availability: All year round.

Vase Life: 2–3 months.

Foliage Notes: Pronounced 'SFAG- num'. A lush, thick moss popular for lining hanging baskets, it occurs primarily in wet habitats where it contributes to the formation of peat bogs.

Colour Range: Cream, pale green with touches of brown and pink.

Conditioning:

- Ideal temperature range: 2–5°C (36–41°F).
- Do not allow to dry out, spray occasionally to keep moist.
- Can be rehydrated if needed by soaking in a bucket of water.
- Store in a plastic bag away from direct heat sources.

General Information:

- Arrives very compact, tease out moss to get maximum volume.
- Wear gloves when handling, removing any twigs or foreign bodies before use.
- Tough and long-lasting, suitable for using in planted designs and floral foam.
- **Texture:** Rough.

 Sphagnum cristatum

In Design and Wedding Work:
This versatile moss has a multitude of uses. Include in textured designs to complement woodland style arrangements and tributes. It can be used as basing material but is not as neat as flat moss or bun moss. Use Sphagnum to cover soil in planted baskets and bowls where its ability to hold water will also benefit the plants. Used for mossing frames before the arrival of floral foam, Sphagnum is still the moss of choice for Christmas holly wreaths and crosses.

For Students:
Family: Sphagnaceae.
Genus & Species: *Sphagnum cristatum*.
Native to: Northern hemisphere.
Trivia: Sphagnum moss is so dense that it can form a thick mat strong enough to support the weight of several moose in its most northerly habitat within the Arctic Circle.

Stachys

Availability: April–June.

Vase Life: 5–7 days.

Foliage Notes: Pronounced 'STACK-is'. An ornamental herbaceous plant with distinctive soft, hairy leaves accompanied by small purple flowers in late spring/early summer. Medium stem length.

Colour Range: Silvery-grey.

Conditioning:

- Ideal temperature range: 2–5°C (36–41°F).
- Re-cut stems and stand in clean water with flower food.
- Ensure no leaves are touching the water.
- Change water every 2–3 days.
- Store away from direct heat and draughts.

General Information:

- Avoid spraying with water as this will spoil the appearance of the leaves.
- Suitable for using in floral foam but will last longer in vase designs.
- **Texture:** Furry.
- **Leaf Shape:** Oval.
- **Would complement:** Delicate, seasonal flowers; Scilla, Ranunculus, Mentha or stocks

 Stachys byzantina

In Design and Wedding Work:

An unusual foliage ideal for adding texture to natural tied posies, woodland style tributes and arrangements. If using in floral foam keep the containers topped up with water, and avoid over-handling as this can take the edge off the leaves. A truly seasonal foliage, use Stachys in informal bridal work where it will enhance soft colour schemes or provide contrast to deeper shades, particularly purples and cerise pinks. Can be wired and glued onto surfaces with care.

For Students:

Family: Lamiaceae.

Genus & Species: *Stachys byzantina*.

Native to: Middle East.

Trivia: A favourite with children who love the feel of its soft, furry leaves. Also sometimes called 'Scouting toilet paper' for reasons that need no further explanation.

Strelitzia

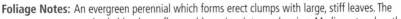

Availability: All year round.

Vase Life: 10–15 days.

Foliage Notes: An evergreen perennial which forms erect clumps with large, stiff leaves. The unmistakable, showy flowers bloom in winter and spring. Medium stem length.

Colour Range: Blue-green.

Conditioning:

- Ideal temperature range: 10–15°C (50–59°F).
- Re-cut stems and stand in clean water with flower food.
- Change water every 4–5 days and mist gently to maintain humidity.
- Leaves are generally packed alongside Strelitzia flowers.
- Store away from direct heat and draughts.

General Information:

- Leaves will gradually curl and split as they age.
- Suitable for using in both vase designs and floral foam.
- **Texture:** Smooth/Ribbed.
- **Leaf Shape:** Oval/Lance.
- **Would complement:** Tropical flowers; Heliconia, Anthurium and of course, Strelitzia

In Design and Wedding Work:

Long-lasting and reliable, Strelitzia leaves lend themselves to large, showy arrangements, particularly in contemporary, structured styles. If using in floral foam, make sure it is well anchored as Strelitzia can be top heavy. Tall vases and hand-ties can be transformed by a few well-placed leaves which will add height and excitement to designs. Obviously the leaves are a trifle over-sized for wedding work, but would be excellent for large modern arrangements in churches and reception venues.

 Strelitzia reginae

For Students:

Family: Strelitziaceae.

Genus & Species: *Strelitzia reginae.*

Native to: South Africa.

Trivia: Strelitzia's flower spathe forms a handy perch for nectar hungry sunbirds. The bird's feet become covered in pollen and as it moves from flower to flower it pollinates in return for its food.

Taxus

Availability: All year round.

Vase Life: 10–21 days.

Foliage Notes: A dense, evergreen tree often found growing in churchyards. Insignificant yellow flowers are followed by fleshy red fruits on female plants in autumn. Medium stem length.

Colour Range: Dark green.

Conditioning:

- Ideal temperature range: 2–5°C (36–41°F).
- Woody stemmed, re-cut with secateurs and stand in clean, fresh water.
- Change water every 3–4 days.
- Store away from direct heat and draughts.
- The fruits contain toxic seeds, wash hands after use.

General Information:

- Remove any foliage in contact with water.
- Suitable for using in both vase designs and floral foam.
- Can substitute with *Tsuga heterophylla* (hemlock).
- **Texture:** Ribbed.
- **Leaf Shape:** Linear.
- **Would complement:** Traditional flowers and Christmas designs.

In Design and Wedding Work:
Not commonly available as commercial cut foliage but one which is reliable and sturdy, excellent for using in the construction of funeral tributes. Large pieces of yew will back tied sheaves and sprays and smaller pieces are great for foliage edging. Useful for swags, garlanding and door wreaths, include it as seasonal foliage in Christmas and winter weddings. Make sure the fruits cannot be reached by inquisitive children and pets. **Foliage meaning:** Sorrow.

 Taxus baccata

For Students:
Family: Taxaceae.
Genus & Species: *Taxus baccata*.
Native to: United Kingdom.
Trivia: Yew was the choice of wood for the longbow, one of the oldest surviving of which was found In Rotten Bottom, Dumfries, Scotland in 1990. Carbon dating revealed it to be 6,000 years old.

Common Name: **Field penny cress, Shepherd's purse**

Availability: All year round, peaks March–November.

Vase Life: 7–14 days.

Foliage Notes: Pronounced 'Th-LAS-pee'. A perennial herb often found growing on roadsides and in meadows. Small and delicate it has off-white flowers in spring and summer. Medium stem length.

Colour Range: Bright green.

Conditioning:

- Ideal temperature range: 2–5°C (36–41°F).
- Re-cut stems and stand in clean water with flower food.
- Change water every 3–5 days.
- Store away from direct heat and draughts.

General Information:

- Handle carefully as the slender stems can bend and damage easily.
- Suitable for using in both vase designs and floral foam.
- **Texture:** Feathery.
- **Would complement:** Delicate spring and summer flowers; Nigella, Mentha, Phlox or Freesia.

Thlaspi 'Green Bell'

In Design and Wedding Work:

Relatively new as a commercially available foliage, Thlaspi fits in beautifully with the trend for all things natural and 'just picked'. It will add a wispy softness to hand-tied bouquets and table arrangements, although its fine, delicate foliage may get overpowered in larger designs. Perfect for informal bridal work and natural tieds it also will fill out vase and jug designs for receptions, and add a light, romantic touch to garlanding and swags. Can be wired with care.

For Students:

Family: Brassicaceae.

Genus & Species: *Thlaspi arvense.*

Native to: Europe, S/W Asia.

Trivia: Regarded by some as a weed, there is evidence of it being a nuisance for crops as far back as Bronze Age times. The seeds are edible and young leaves can be added to salads.

Thymus

Common Name: **Garden thyme, Common thyme**

Availability: April–October.

Vase Life: 5–7 days.

Foliage Notes: Pronounced 'TIE-mus'. A bushy, evergreen herb with small, strongly aromatic leaves. Tiny pink or white flowers appear in late spring and summer. Short stem length.

Colour Range: Green-grey to bright green.

Conditioning:

- Ideal temperature range: 2–5°C (36–41°F).
- Re-cut stems and stand in clean water with flower food.
- Ensure no leaves are touching the water.
- Woody stemmed, change water every 2–3 days.
- Store away from direct heat and draughts.

Thymus vulgaris

General Information:

- Do not eat thyme grown commercially for the cut flower market.
- Suitable for using in both vase designs and floral foam.
- **Texture:** Bushy.
- **Leaf Shape:** Oval.
- **Would complement:** Delicate summer flowers; Astrantia, Bouvardia, Forget-me-not.

In Design and Wedding Work:

A lovely herb to add into natural and informal tied posies and petite vase designs. Too short stemmed for large arrangements its delicate form lends itself to smaller, more intimate work. For brides looking for very natural garden flowers, thyme is ideal especially when combined with other herbs such as mint and oregano, but be careful that the scent of so many aromatic herbs on a hot day doesn't become too overpowering! Can be used in wired work.

Foliage meaning: Activity.

For Students:

Family: Lamiaceae.

Genus & Species: *Thymus vulgaris.*

Native to: Mediterranean.

Trivia: An essential herb in medicine and cooking; in the Middle Ages sprigs of thyme were placed under pillows to ward off nightmares and aid sleep.

Common Name: **Spanish moss, Spanish beard**

Availability: All year round.

Vase Life: Indefinite.

Foliage Notes: Despite its common name Tillandsia is not a true moss. Its slender, branching stems hang from trees forming a dense curtain which can grow up to 6m (20') long.

Colour Range: Pale green to silver-grey.

Conditioning:

- Ideal temperature range: 2–5°C (36–41°F).
- Spray occasionally to keep up humidity and prevent it from drying out.
- Do not leave soaking in water.
- Store away from direct heat and cold draughts.
- Do not store for long periods in the dark.

General Information:

- Fresh Tillandsia is pale green; it turns grey as it dries out.
- Suitable for using in both vase designs and floral foam.
- Texture: Stringy.
- Would complement:
  Delicate flowers in neutral and pastel colour combinations.

 Tillandsia usneoides

In Design and Wedding Work:
Although it has the appearance of an unravelling vest, Tillandsia is very effective in modern, structured designs where it can be suspended from frameworks, echoing it natural state. It is also very easy to pin and wire into floral foam, both in fresh and artificial designs. Use Tillandsia in textured work and as an alternative to traditional basing materials. It would not look out of place in bridal showers if used with a degree of restraint.

For Students:
Family: Bromeliaceae.
Genus & Species: *Tillandsia usneoides.*
Native to: S/E United States.
Trivia: Tillandsia propagates mainly by wind borne fragments that lodge in trees. This causes a problem in the hurricane season as its density increases the trees wind resistance.

Tillandsia

Common Name: **Air plant**

Availability: All year round.

Vase Life: Indefinite.

Foliage Notes: A fascinating plant which inhabits dry forest and scrubland, growing on the highest branches where light is brightest. It has a striking, brightly coloured flower which can last for months. Short stem length.

Colour Range: Pale green to silvery-grey.

Conditioning:

- Ideal temperature range: 7–15°C (44–59°F).
- Mist gently, once or twice a week.
- Handle with care and do not let it stand in water.
- Has no need for moss or compost.
- Store away from direct heat and cold draughts.

 Tillandsia xerographica

General Information:

- To keep it at its best, place in a concave bowl with good air circulation.
- **Texture:** Smooth.
- **Leaf Shape:** Lance.
- **Would complement:** Tall structures, vegetative designs and static displays.

In Design and Wedding Work:
The beautiful sculptural form of this unusual plant would complement stripped back designs where every flower and foliage has its own place. Attach to branches and frameworks or use to enhance a focal area. Perfect for textured work. Use in contemporary bridal designs by either including the whole plant or detaching individual leaves and wiring or gluing into shower and cascade bouquets. Its longevity also makes it great for shop and window displays.

For Students:
Family: Bromeliaceae.
Genus & Species: *Tillandsia xerographica*.
Native to: Central America.
Trivia: *Tillandsia xerographica* is grown commercially for the floristry and interior design industries. In the wild it is protected by CITES (Convention on International Trade in Endangered Species).

Triticum

Common Name: **Wheat**

Availability: November–July, peaks December–June.

Vase Life: 5–7 days fresh. Can also be dried.

Foliage Notes: An annual grass, one of several species of cultivated wheat grown worldwide. Flowering in June and July, its seeds ripen in late summer/early autumn. Medium stem length.

Colour Range: Pale green to parchment shades when dried.

Conditioning:

- Ideal temperature range: 2–5°C (36–41°F).
- Re-cut stems and stand in clean water with flower food.
- Change water every 2–3 days and don't overcrowd containers.
- Store away from direct heat and draughts.

General Information:

- Commercially dried wheat is easier to obtain than fresh.
- Fresh or dried it is suitable for using in both vase designs and floral foam.
- **Texture:** Rough.
- **Leaf Shape:** Lance.
- **Would complement:** Summer and autumn flowers; Nigella, Carthamus, Papaver or cornflowers

 Triticum aestivum

In Design and Wedding Work:

Whether dried or fresh adding wheat into designs gives an instant flavour of seasonality. Include fresh green wheat in natural hand-tieds and arrangements, group together for more impact. Dried wheat is perfect for autumn weddings, combine it with berries and seed heads in bridal work, vase designs and venue arrangements. Suitable for using in wired work, dried wheat can also be sprayed gold and silver and used in Christmas designs. **Foliage Meaning:** Riches.

For Students:

Family: Poaceae.

Genus & Species: *Triticum aestivum.*

Native to: Mediterranean & S/W Asia.

Trivia: Wheat is an ancient crop; there is evidence of it being cultivated as far back as 9,600 BC. Today, wheat is grown on 4% of the Earth's agricultural land.

Typha

Common Name: **Lesser bulrush, Narrow reed-mace**

Availability: July–September.

Vase Life: 5–7 days.

Foliage Notes: Found growing on the margins of watery habitats, the velvety cylindrical flower spikes of the bulrush are unmistakable. Medium/tall stem length.

Colour Range: Chocolate brown.

Conditioning:

- Ideal temperature range: 2–5°C (36–41°F).
- Re-cut stems and stand in clean, shallow water.
- Change water every 2–3 days.
- Store away from direct heat and draughts.

General Information:

- Suitable for using in both vase designs and floral foam.
- Don't overcrowd containers or vases, it needs good air circulation.
- **Texture:** Velvety.
- **Leaf Shape:** Strap.
- **Would complement:** Tall, bold flowers; Knifophia, Dahlia, or Helianthus

In Design and Wedding Work:

Tall, erect stems of bulrush work incredibly well in modern, structured designs. Use them to add drama to large arrangements, grouping them together for maximum impact. Ideally suited for textured and vegetative arrangements, they are also very useful for competition work. Great for using in corporate designs, their only disadvantage is that they can 'burst' as they mature spreading fluffy seeds, so only use the freshest bulrushes for restaurants and public areas!

 Typha angustifolia

For Students:

Family: Typhaceae.

Genus & Species: *Typha angustifolia*.

Native to: Americas, Europe & Africa.

Trivia: Parts of *T. angustifolia* are edible, including the starchy roots, the ripe pollen and the inner core of the stalk. The edible stem is known as *bồn bồn* in Vietnam.

Typha

Availability: March–December.

Vase Life: 10–21 days.

Foliage Notes: A deciduous perennial which can be found growing in dense clumps on the margins of ponds and other watery habitats. Medium/tall stem length.

Colour Range: Mid-green.

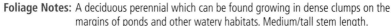

Conditioning:

- Ideal temperature range: 2–5°C (36–41°F).
- Re-cut stems and stand in clean water with flower food.
- Change water every 4–5 days.
- Store away from direct heat and draughts.

General Information:

- Suitable for using in both vase designs and floral foam.
- **Texture:** Smooth.
- **Leaf Shape:** Strap.
- **Would complement:** Tropical flowers such as orchids, Curcuma or Anthurium

In Design and Wedding Work:

Indispensable in modern floristry, Typha grass is hugely versatile, particularly in wedding work, where it can be looped, woven and knotted into bridal bouquets, hand-tied posies and elaborate wired designs. Lengths of Typha create a natural screen to which flower heads, berries and decorative beads can be attached. It is also flexible enough to wrap around vases and frameworks and to form a natural collar around hand-ties. Lengths of Typha can be wired together to create three dimensional structures.

Typha latifolia

For Students:

Family: Typhaceae.

Genus & Species: *Typha latifolia.*

Native to: Northern hemisphere.

Trivia: Always found by water or exposed mud, *T. latifolia* spreads by wind dispersing it fruits and has become more prevalent in boggy areas in the last forty years.

141

Vaccinium

Common Name: **Bilberry, Whortleberry**

Availability: October–May, peaks November–April.

Vase Life: 14–21 days.

Foliage Notes: Pronounced 'Vac-SIN-e-um'. An evergreen shrub that grows wild on heathlands and acidic soils. Small bell-shaped flowers are followed in autumn by edible, juicy berries. Medium stem length.

Colour Range: Mid-green.

Conditioning:

- Ideal temperature range: 2–5°C (36–41°F).
- Re-cut stems and stand in clean water.
- Change water every 4–5 days.
- Store away from direct heat and draughts.

General Information:

- Woody stemmed, long-lasting foliage, hardy and resilient.
- Suitable for using in both vase designs and floral foam.
- **Texture:** Spiky.
- **Would complement:** Suitable for both traditional and spring flowers.

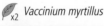 *Vaccinium myrtillus*

In Design and Wedding Work:
Not a stylish foliage but one which is extremely useful as filler in hand-tieds and arrangements. Very flexible and robust, it can be wired into bundles and used to add texture and bulk to designs. Vaccinium takes spray paint very well, so is handy for Christmas arrangements when sprayed gold or silver. Wire into garlanding and swags to add a spiky contrast and extra volume at very little cost. **Foliage meaning:** Treachery.

For Students:
Family: Ericaceae.
Genus & Species: *Vaccinium myrtillus.*
Native to: Northern Europe.
Trivia: Bilberries are used in both herbal medicine and cooking, they can be picked and eaten raw – but beware – they can stain fingers and teeth bright purple!

Viburnum

Common Name: **Viburnum, Laurustinus**

Availability: October–March.

Vase Life: 7–14 days.

Foliage Notes: A bushy evergreen shrub, popular in landscaping schemes. It bears clusters of pink buds which open into small, fragrant, star-shaped flowers. Medium stem length.

Colour Range: Dark green.

Conditioning:

- Ideal temperature range: 2–5°C (36–41°F).
- Re-cut stems and stand in clean water with flower food.
- Change water every 4–5 days.
- Store away from direct heat and draughts.

General Information:

- Woody stemmed, reliable and long-lasting foliage.
- Suitable for using in both vase designs and floral foam.
- **Texture:** Smooth.
- **Leaf Shape:** Oval.
- **Would complement:** Traditional autumn and winter flowers.

🌿x2 *Viburnum tinus* 'Eve Price'

In Design and Wedding Work:

Viburnum's bushy form makes it ideal for filling out large, traditional arrangements and for giving volume to funeral sprays and hand-tied bouquets. Not striking or individual enough for modern, contemporary work however. If using Viburnum whilst in flower it will provide a pretty, delicate background to bolder flowers in natural tied posies and informal vase designs. Can be used in wired work with care.

For Students:

Family: Adoxaceae.

Genus & Species: *Viburnum tinus.*

Native to: Mediterranean.

Trivia: *Pyrrhalta viburni*, or Viburnum leaf beetle, is a pest native to Europe and Asia which eats away at Viburnum leaves until the plant is skeletonised. The RHS call it 'number one pest species'.

143

Viburnum

Common Name: **Viburnum, Pepper berries**

Availability: September–May.

Vase Life: 7–14 days.

Foliage Notes: This bushy shrub grows as a compact dome which makes it suitable for most gardens. The berries appear after the flowers have finished in late summer. Medium stem length.

Colour Range: Steel blue.

Conditioning:

- Ideal temperature range: 2–5°C (36–41°F).
- Re-cut stems and stand in clean water with flower food.
- Change water every 4–5 days.
- Store away from direct heat and draughts.

General Information:

- Woody stemmed, reliable and long-lasting foliage.
- Suitable for using in both vase designs and floral foam.
- **Texture:** Shiny.
- **Leaf Shape:** Oval.
- **Would complement:** Delicate flowers; Hellebore, Anemone or spray roses.

Viburnum tinus 'Eve Price'

In Design and Wedding Work:

The unusual steel blue colour of these berries adds an interesting contrast to designs. Most effective in hand-tied bouquets and vase arrangements where they can be appreciated as they are liable to get overpowered in larger, more flamboyant work. Lovely for autumn and spring weddings, in bridal designs these berries can be used on their natural stems in informal hand-ties or wired and added into more structured shower bouquets, buttonholes and corsages.

For Students:

Family: Adoxaceae.

Genus & Species: *Viburnum tinus.*

Native to: Mediterranean.

Trivia: The fruits of Viburnum are sometimes used a purgative, although it is generally advised not to consume them as they can cause stomach upsets.

Viscum

Availability: November–December.

Vase Life: 5–7 days.

Foliage Notes: Often spotted growing in the crowns of trees in winter, mistletoe attaches itself to branches where it absorbs nutrients from its unwitting host. Medium stem length.

Colour Range: Sage green with milky white berries.

Conditioning:

- Ideal temperature range: 2–5°C (36–41°F).
- Storing mistletoe outside in cold temperatures will prolong its life.
- Wash hands after use.
- If storing in water, change it every 2–3 days.
- Store away from direct heat and cold draughts.

General Information:

- Traditionally sold 'dry' in bundles.
- Look for plump berries, withered berries mean the plant is old.
- **Texture:** Smooth.
- **Leaf Shape:** Lance.
- **Would complement:** Christmas foliage and flowers.

Viscum album

In Design and Wedding Work:

Although mistletoe traditionally ends up suspended from ceilings at parties, it is great seasonal foliage which is often overlooked in design work. Pretty hand-tied posies and seasonal vases can be enhanced by including mistletoe; it can also be added into garlands and swags. If using in wedding work be wary of the berries which can stain if squashed, for this reason not suitable for wiring work. Mistletoe will last longer in outdoor displays than in the warm indoors.

Foliage meaning: I surmount difficulties.

For Students:

Family: Santalaceae.

Genus & Species: *Viscum album.*

Native to: Europe & Asia.

Trivia: Found most commonly in apple, lime, hawthorn, poplar and oak trees. Druids believe that mistletoe collected from oak has special properties.

Weigela

Common Name: **Weigela**

Availability: June–November, peaks July–October.

Vase Life: 5–7 days.

Foliage Notes: Pronounced 'We-GEE-le-a'. A bushy deciduous shrub and a common sight in many gardens. Attractive and easy to grow, it bears funnel-shaped flowers in summer. Medium stem length.

Colour Range: Mid-green, often variegated.

Conditioning:

- Ideal temperature range: 2–5°C (36–41°F).
- Re-cut stems and stand in clean water with flower food.
- Remove any leaves that might be in contact with water.
- Change water every 2–3 days.
- Store away from direct heat and draughts.

General Information:

- Do not overcrowd vases or containers.
- Weigela will wilt quickly if left out of water.
- **Texture:** Bushy.
- **Leaf Shape:** Oval.
- **Would complement:**
  Traditional cottage
  garden summer flowers.

 Weigela florida foliis Purpureis

In Design and Wedding Work:

A useful, bushy foliage which looks great in large scale traditional designs or natural hand-tieds. A good filler, although it has a tendency to dry out quickly if left out of water for any length of time, so if using in floral foam make sure containers are kept topped up. Good for vase designs, funeral tributes and tied sheaves its variegated foliage will add colour and texture to arrangements. A little too traditional for more contemporary work. Not suitable for wiring.

For Students:

Family: Caprifoliaceae.

Genus & Species: *Weigela florida.*

Native to: Eastern Asia.

Trivia: Introduced into England in 1845 by Scottish botanist Robert Fortune, who is better remembered for successfully introducing tea plants from China to India.

Xanthorrhoea

Common Name: **Steel grass, Southern grass tree**

Availability: All year round.

Vase Life: 10–21 days.

Foliage Notes: Pronounced 'Zan-thor-ROH-ee-a'. Tall, straight grass which grows as large tufts on trees growing on sandy soils and rocky hillsides. Fire tolerant, it relies on intense heat to stimulate growth. Tall stem length.

Colour Range: Green with a silver sheen.

Conditioning:

- Ideal temperature range: 2–5°C (36–41°F).
- Re-cut stems with scissors or a sharp knife.
- Stand in clean water with flower food.
- Change water every 5–6 days.
- Store away from direct heat and draughts.

General Information:

- Handle carefully to avoid grass cuts.
- Brown ends can be trimmed off.
- Suitable for using in both vase designs and floral foam.
- **Texture:** Spiky.
- **Leaf Shape:** Linear.
- **Would complement:** Tall flowers; Strelitzia, Anthurium or Heliconia.

In Design and Wedding Work:

A versatile grass which is excellent for giving height and linear interest to large designs. Although ideal for modern arrangements, it will not look out of place in more traditional work, but be careful if adding into designs in public places as wayward steel grass can be quite dangerous! Not flexible enough to be woven or knotted, it can however be 'cracked' to create angles to add a geometric dimension to designs. It is also strong enough to thread berries, fruits and flowers onto.

 Xanthorrhoea australis

For Students:

Family: Xanthorrhoeaceae.

Genus & Species: *Xanthorrhoea australis.*

Native to: Australia.

Trivia: Extremely slow growing, around 1–3cm a year, Xanthorrhoea can live for over 300 years. It is a staple plant for Aborigines, providing food, drink and materials for tools.

Xerophyllum

Availability: All year round.

Vase Life: 7–14 days.

Foliage Notes: Pronounced 'Zer-OH-phil-um'. A hardy grass capable of surviving forest fires whose tightly bunched flowers emerge in late spring/early summer. Medium stem length.

Colour Range: Olive green.

Conditioning:

- Ideal temperature range: 2–5°C (36–41°F).
- Re-cut stems with scissors and stand in clean water with flower food.
- Do not undo bunches, change water every 3–4 days.
- Store away from direct heat and draughts which will cause the blades to curl.

General Information:

- Watch out for grass cuts – handle with care.
- Brown ends can be trimmed off.
- Suitable for using in both vase designs and floral foam.
- **Texture:** Spiky.
- **Leaf Shape:** Linear.
- **Would complement:** Practically all flowers, except for very tall stems.

In Design and Wedding Work:

Incredibly versatile, bear grass is equally at home in modern or traditional designs. It will add linear movement to hand-tieds and its arching stems will enhance designs in floral foam. Use this flexible grass as a 'bridge' to link points of interest together and to emphasise focal points. In wedding work it is lovely in natural posies and it is easy to loop and cut into segments to complement wired buttonholes and corsages. Strong enough to glue berries and flowers onto.

Xerophyllum tenax

For Students:

Family: Melianthaceae.

Genus & Species: *Xerophyllum tenax.*

Native to: North America.

Trivia: Used extensively by Native Americans who used this tough grass to make baskets and garments and who would also roast and eat the root stock.

Yucca

Availability: All year round.

Vase Life: 7–14 days.

Foliage Notes: An evergreen shrub popular in landscaping schemes. Its stiff leaves grow in a rosette shape which produces a tall panicle of bell-shaped flowers in late summer. Medium stem length.

Colour Range: Blue-green.

Conditioning:

- Ideal temperature range: 12–15°C (54–59°F).
- Re-cut stems and stand in clean water with flower food.
- Change water every 4–5 days.
- Store away from direct heat and draughts.

General Information:

- Avoid spraying with water as this can mark the surface.
- For safety's sake, snip off the tip of the leaf before using.
- Store above head height to avoid possible injury from the sharp points of the leaves.
- **Texture:** Smooth.
- **Leaf Shape:** Sword.
- **Would complement:** Tall, tropical flowers; Heliconia, Strelitzia and Anthurium.

In Design and Wedding Work:
Specialised foliage more likely to be seen in competition work than in your everyday arrangement. Striking and individual, Yucca will stand out whether used singly or in a group. If adding into floral foam, ensure it is well anchored in; it is less successful in vase designs and hand-tieds where it can be a little unwieldy. It can be used vertically or horizontally and is tough enough to be hollowed or drilled into to support smaller flowers or attachments.

 Yucca gloriosa

For Students:
Family: Asparagaceae.
Genus & Species: Yucca gloriosa.
Native to: Southern USA.
Trivia: Often found growing in between graves in the Midwest USA where it is known as 'ghosts in graveyards' as the tall, cream flower spikes appear as floating apparitions at certain times of the day.

Zea

Common Name: **Ornamental corn, Maize**

Availability: August–December.

Vase Life: Indefinite.

Foliage Notes: The unmistakeable leafy stalks of corn are recognisable worldwide. Sweetcorn is grown for human consumption, field corn for cattle feed. Short/medium stem length.

Colour Range: Creamy yellow, maroon, chestnut brown.

Conditioning:

- Zea arrives already dried so no further conditioning is needed.
- Ideal temperature range: 2–5°C (36–41°F).
- Store/display in a dry area.
- Store away from direct heat, damp and draughts.

General Information:

- Avoid spraying with water.
- Suitable for using in both vase designs and floral foam.
- Can be sprayed with paint.
- **Texture:** Rippled.
- **Would complement:** Textured autumn and Christmas flowers and foliages.

 Zea mays

In Design and Wedding Work:

Dried corn is an ideal material for floral decorations in the latter part of the year. Combine them with dried chillies and capsicum and wire them into door wreaths and swags at harvest time, Halloween and Christmas. If they have been left on their stems they are great for adding texture to vase designs and arrangements in floral foam, although avoid getting the dried outer leaves wet as they go mouldy easily. Lovely for setting the scene at autumn weddings and harvest festivals.

For Students:

Family: Poaceae.

Genus & Species: *Zea mays.*

Native to: Central America.

Trivia: Able to grow in a diverse range of climates, corn has been cultivated since prehistoric times. It first came to Europe in the 15th century via European explorers.

A mini foliage miscellany

Foliage 'fo-liage. A cluster of leaves; plant leaves considered as a group' from the Latin 'folium' meaning 'leaf'.

Leaf Shapes

In botany, there are over 60 different shapes of leaves, below are the ones which are most commonly come across and which appear in this book.

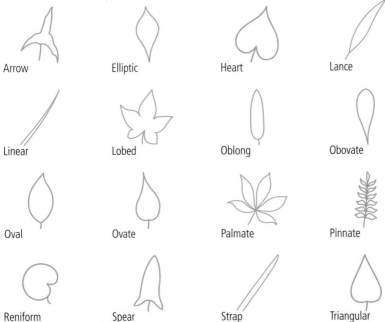

Arrow   Elliptic   Heart   Lance

Linear   Lobed   Oblong   Obovate

Oval   Ovate   Palmate   Pinnate

Reniform   Spear   Strap   Triangular

Some fascinating foliage facts!

The largest leaf is that of the raffia palm (*Raphia regalis*) it has pinnate leaves that are capable of growing up to 24m (80')

Conversely, the smallest leaf is that of the common water fern, *Azolla filiculoides*, a mere 1mm in length.

The Maple leaf is the National symbol of Canada, added into the Canadian coat of arms in 1921. Canada's flag is the only national flag to feature a leaf.

The Arctic willow (*Salix arctica*) is the world's most northerly woody plant. Growing within the Arctic Circle, it rarely exceeds heights of 15cm (6') and is incredibly slow growing; one in Eastern Greenland was found to be 236 years old.

Glossary

Botanical and floristry terms

Annual	A plant that completes its entire life cycle in one year.
Basing	Also massed/blocked. Flower material bonded closely together to create a larger whole.
Boutonnière	A selection of small flowers arranged to create a buttonhole normally worn by a bridegroom.
Buttonhole	A flower backed with foliage and often augmented with buds, berries, decorative wires and pins.
Corsage	Flowers and foliage arranged into a design suitable to be worn on a lapel, handbag, wrist or hat.
Deciduous	A plant which annually sheds its foliage at the end of its growing season.
Decorative material	Non-floral materials, such as pins, coloured wires, diamante and beads.
Edging	Foliage or ribbon wired or pinned to the outer edge of a tribute to form a border.
Epiphytic	A plant which depends on another for support, but not nutrients.
Ethylene gas	A colourless, odourless gas produced by plants, fruits and vegetables as they ripen.
Evergreen	A plant which keeps its foliage throughout the year.
Family	A closely related group of flowers and plants sharing common characteristics.
Filler foliage	A bushy foliage which can be used to 'fill' out arrangements and bouquets.
Floral foam	Commercially produced medium for holding fresh or dried flowers or foliage in place.
Flower food	Commercially produced powder or liquid designed to improve and extend vase life.
Focal	The most prominent part in an arrangement that the eye is automatically drawn to.
Foliage	The leaves of a plant or a cluster of leaves seen as a group.
Framework	Placement of materials outside of the focal area to form a supporting structure.
Garlanding	Lengths of foliage and/or flowers that are hung for decoration. Can be several metres in length.
Genus	A subdivision of flowers or plants within a larger family that closely resemble each other.
Hand-tied	A selection of natural flowers and foliage arranged in a spiral, creating an all-round design.
Herbaceous plant	A plant lacking a woody stem, whose above ground growth dies down in winter.
Houseplant	An ornamental/decorative plant, flowering and/or green which is grown indoors.
Humidity	The level of moisture/water vapour in the air.

Botanical and floristry terms

Inflorescence	The complete flower head of a plant, including stems, stalks and flowers.
Latex	A milky, sometimes sticky sap exuded by certain plants.
Leaf shine	A commercial spray designed to give an artificial gloss to leaves.
Lichen	A fungus which forms a branching or crust like growth on rocks or trees.
Linear	A design in which lines – vertical, horizontal or curved – are the most dominant form.
Natural tied posy	Small headed flowers on natural stems arranged in a spiral often carried by a child.
Pedestal design	A large arrangement standing on a base suitable for a church or reception venue.
Perennial	A plant that has a life cycle of three or more seasons.
Sap	Fluid that circulates through a plant, carrying food and other substances to the various tissues.
Shower bouquet	A formal tear-drop shaped bridal bouquet either wired or arranged in a holder of floral foam.
Shrub	A plant with a woody stem and which is usually branched from the base upwards.
Soft stemmed	A plant with a non-woody stem.
Structured design	An arrangement either hand-tied or in floral foam with limited flower material and bold, clean cut lines, often designed within a framework.
Succulent	A plant that has thick, fleshy leaves.
Swag	Material either tied naturally or mounted on a base that is used as a door or wall hanging.
Synonymous (Syn)	A plant known by two botanical names that share the same characteristics.
Textural	A design that has both visual and physical texture.
Traditional	A design in a recognised geometric form with materials radiating from a focal area, with flower materials grouped according to colour and form.
Tribute	Flower material arranged as a design suitable for a funeral, i.e. as a cross, heart or spray.
Tropical foliage	Foliage from the tropic areas that typically thrive in hot and humid conditions.
Variegation	Leaves containing two or more colours.
Vegetative	Flower and plant material used in its original method of growth, i.e. vertical or trailing.
Wiring/wired work	Flowers and foliage that have been individually wired to create a buttonhole, corsage or other floral decoration worn usually for weddings and formal occasions.
Woody stemmed	A stem composed of woody fibres which doesn't die down over winter.

Index

Common names

Common names

Acknowledgements...

...and thanks

The author would like to acknowledge the following organizations and sources of reference:

The Royal Horticultural Society Gardener's Encyclopedia of Plants and Flowers

RHS Plant Selector (rhs.org.uk)

Royal Botanic Gardens Kew

Flower Council of Holland

Foliage for Florists, Society of Floristry

Foliage and Plants for Flower Arranging, NAFAS

The Houseplant Expert, Dr. D.G. Hessayon

A Field Guide to the Trees of Britain and Northern Europe, Alan Mitchell

Plantzafrica www.plantzafrica.com

Dave's Garden www.davesgarden.com

My grateful thanks go out to:

Photographer Mark Follon, who once again took charge of boxes of 'twigs' (his description) sent to him over the months and produced such excellent photography.

Janet Bowyer and all at Corner House Design & Print for their hard work over and above the call of duty in producing this book.

Brett Whale O.N.D. Arb for tree advice and for being a willing sounding board.

Kathryn Barker, Doncaster College, Tina Parks, Academy of Floral Art, Joan Hutchings Capel Manor College and Alison Johnson, Rodbaston College.

Joy Gill and Mandy Davis at the Flower Centre, Northfield –for sourcing so much of the foliage and for being so understanding. Jennifer Bills for lending me her coursework, Alison Bradley from Fusion Flowers for her eternal enthusiasm and support. All the people who raided their gardens for me and last, but not least, Mr Phil O'Dendron for keeping the pages in order.